The Ten Week Garden

The Ten Week Garden
by Cary Scher

Illustrated and hand lettered by Linda Larisch

Something Else Press
Barton, Vermont, 1973

L.C. Card Catalog No.: 73-76848
ISBN: 0-87110-101-7

Copyright© 1973 by Something
Else Press, Inc., P.O. Box 26, West Glover,
Vt. 05875. All rights reserved. No
portion whatever of this text may be
reproduced in any form except for
brief passages quoted for inclusion
in a review written for a magazine
or a newspaper or radio or television
broadcast.

Manufactured in the United States
of America.

dedicated
to Linda, my wife

and a special thanks
to Dick Higgins for his confidence

Contents

Introduction 1
Soils 9
Drainage 14
Selecting a Site 16
Testing the Soil 18
Compost 23
Manure 32
Mulches 37
Fertilizers 44
Starting Seeds Early 48
Our Garden Plan 54
Coldframes & Hotbeds 55
Preparing the Soil 63
Water 66
Cultivating & Weeding 68
Insect & Disease Control 71
Artichoke, Jerusalem 78
Asparagus 86
Beans 96
Beets 106
Broccoli 114
Brussels Sprouts 121
Cabbage 128
Carrots 135

Cauliflower 142
Celery + Celeriac 149
Celtuce 157
Chard, Swiss 160
Chicory 165
Chinese Cabbage 169
Collards 175
Corn 178
Corn Salad 190
Cucumbers 193
Eggplant 205
Endive 213
Herbs 219
Horseradish 237
Kale 243
Kohlrabi 250
Leeks 255
Lettuce 262
Marijuana 275
Melons 281
Mustards 290
The Onion Family 294
Parsnips 308
Peas 313
Peppers 323
Potatoes 332

Radish 343
Rhubarb 349
Salsify 355
Spinach 358
Squash & Pumpkins 363
Strawberries 372
Tomatoes 384
Turnips + Rutabagas 394
Planting Chart 400
Sources of Supply 402
Selected Bibliography . . 406

Introduction

There are perhaps forty million reasons for having a garden, one for each of the approximate forty million gardeners in America. In this book I have tried to describe the newest techniques of gardening, as well as the basic fundamentals, so that anyone may acquire a "green thumb". The myth of the green thumb is nothing more than Knowing what to do and doing it at the right time.

Organic gardening is not really new. Nature has been the best organic gardener of all and man has always grown his food this way until recently. But modern man is all too quick to spray deadly poisons on his food as soon as he sees an insect. No garden is completely free of insects, nor should it be. A garden is a place of refuge for all Kinds of life. It is no place for poisons. By following sound organic practices the need for the flit gun will never arise.

Gardening is not something that stays the same, there is nothing static about it. Continuous birth, death, and rebirth puts one in close and constant touch with Nature. We don't always understand her, but there is most surely a lesson to be learned.

Commercial vegetable growers are only interested in getting the largest yield and in making the most money from the land, with little regard for the environment or the quality of the food. In other words, land rape. They have relied mainly on the synthetic or chemical fertilizers to to keep production up. Meanwhile the country is being polluted with disposal of organic wastes in the wrong places when it should be returned to the soil. Soil fertility and healthy people go hand in hand! We cannot expect to continually harvest the land without returning organic matter to the soil and still reap the good life.

Even if you live in the far, far North and are faced with the prospects of gardening on permafrost, where the soil thaws to a depth of only 15 inches, don't think it can't be done. With some extra effort and a prudent choice of the hardiest early maturing varieties, a successful garden can be grown even in the Arctic Circle. Cold country gardeners have invented all sorts of tricks to help bring plants to maturity. Raised planting beds, portable cold frames, and small, individual greenhouses help to extend a growing season of sometimes only 50 days. So there is no such thing as being too far north to garden.

Gardening here in Vermont is also especially challenging. There was one year I remember when a frost occurred every month. But despite the short season, we have been able to grow all our yearly vegetable needs in this most

uncooperative climate. We have
seen our clay soil come
alive by following basic
organic gardening principles
of mulching, fertilizing,
and composting, plus a few
tricks of our own.
          Our garden is not
large by most standards.
It is about 40' x 50' (2,000 sq. ft.).
But a small well-kept garden
can be surprisingly productive.
Once your soil has reached
a state of high fertility,
you don't really need a
large garden. By careful
planning, we sometimes even
produce more than we can
use. We manage to have a
50 ft. row of asparagus and
a small patch of strawberries,
also flowers and herbs.
A small garden allows you

to inspect every plant, no space need be wasted.

Compost and manure go much further too. You can really put them on lavishly in a small area and production will amaze you. So, my advise is to start small. As you gain experience you can always increase the size of your garden. Naturally, what you grow depends upon what you like, but also on space considerations, so keep in mind that some vegetables yield more for the space they occupy than others. For example, cabbage gives you four times as much food as corn or asparagus will for the same area.

If you have never

eaten food fresh from the garden, you will be in for a special treat, since some vegetables like corn, peas, and asparagus, should be picked just before eating — any other way falls short of perfection. But garden fresh vegetables are not enough. They must be gathered in their prime, and only a kitchen garden assures this.

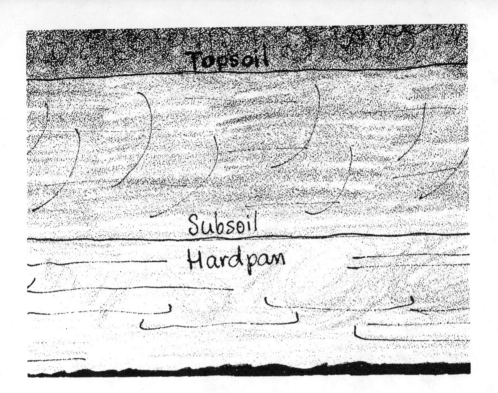

Topsoil

Subsoil

Hardpan

Soils

Soil is the home for your plants. Soils are classed according to the amount of clay and sand they contain. Clay is so finely textured the particles are extremely small. It feels smooth when you rub it between your fingers. But sand particles can be seen and felt individually. A sandy soil dries out quicker than clay and makes it possible to plant much earlier in the Spring.

Clay - less than $\frac{1}{12,000}$ inch

Silt - $\frac{1}{12,000}$ to $\frac{1}{500}$ inch

Fine Sand - $\frac{1}{500}$ to $\frac{1}{250}$ inch

medium sand - $\frac{1}{100}$ to $\frac{1}{50}$ inch

Coarse Sand - $\frac{1}{2}$ inch

Combinations of sand and clay with organic matter are called loams. This is the most desirable type of soil because it combines the best qualities of each. It is easier to work and it warms up earlier in the spring.

Clay soils hold more moisture than sandy soils but are a lot harder to prepare. Clay soils have the advantage of not wasting nutrients.

When you start a new garden you have to take what's there and try continually to improve it. Your goal should be increased fertility and production. These goals have been achieved in places like Japan and China where the same piece of land has been under continuous cultivation for thousands of years. Instead of always taking from the soil, they try to put back more than they take from it. This should be our goal. Every scrap of organic matter is returned to the soil where it belongs. Farmers in Japan have even set up roadside toilets for travelers to use, so they may collect the human excrement to return it to the land. However, this is not recommended because it has been found that unless properly handled, human wastes can be a source of intestinal parasites.

Farmers in the United States and other places have not followed the example of their oriental brothers and the results have been disastrous. The use of more and stronger chemical fertilizers and pesticides have taken the place of composts

and manures but soils do not
support normal plant growth
without organic matter. This
has led to a marked decrease
in the health and vitality of
the people who are forced to
eat this food.

Because of this narrow-
minded attitude more and more
people have decided to try their
hand at gardening organically.

Drainage

Almost all soils can be improved. If your soil is a heavy clay you can add peat moss, sand, and organic matter, which will make it lighter and permit more air to enter, improving the drainage. Wet soils that stay wet are poorly drained.

Sometimes the only solution, if we are faced with such a soil, is to install artificial drainage. Drainage of the soil by means of drain tiles and ditches is a last resort if no other suitable land is available.

Our first garden was in a low place where water collected and almost nothing thrived. The solution was simple. We moved our garden to a higher piece of land the next year and everything improved.

Good drainage removes the excess water and allows the air to enter the soil. Air in the soil is important for the beneficial organisms, such as aerobic bacteria and fungi, which help in the breakdown of organic matter. This decomposition of organic matter makes the nutrients available to the plants.

Sandy soils are naturally better drained than the heavier soils and they are more valuable in growing earlier crops.

Selecting a Site

Poorly drained soils should be avoided unless no other site is available. Another thing to look for when selecting a garden site is an abundance of sun. The ideal place would recieve sun the full day.

However, most vegetables would do well if they receive 6 to 8 hours of sun each day. Try to keep the site away from large trees which would not only shade the garden but would take water and nutrients away from the vegetables.

One more point to keep in mind when selecting a site: try to keep the garden as close to the house as possible. It is a simple matter to get a sprig of parsley or a carrot for your salad when you only have to walk a few steps. But a long walk might make you forego that pleasure.

Weeds are indicators of fertility. Take a close look at the site you have chosen. Notice what's growing there. Are the weeds dark green? Sturdy? Lush? Or are they pale, yellow, and scrawny. Just holding their own? It is not that important to identify all the weeds by name, although it would be helpful. Try to pick a place that is naturally rich and you're off to a much better start. If you see dandelions growing on your site you can be sure the soil will grow fine vegetables with a little help from you.

Testing the Soil

You might want to have your soil tested to check on the plant foods it contains. Several easy-to-use, inexpensive kits are available and do a good job. The Sudbury is one. Or soil samples can be sent to your state agricultural experimental college to be tested for one or two dollars. But ignore their recommendations for chemical fertilizers.

One of the things a test would indicate is the acidity/alkalinity of your soil. This is expressed as the pH factor. The pH starts at zero which is the most acid and goes to fourteen which is the most alkaline. Seven is considered

PH scale

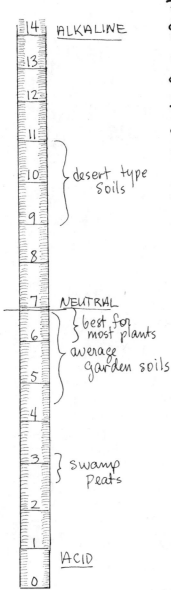

ALKALINE — 14, 13, 12, 11

desert type Soils — 10, 9, 8

NEUTRAL — 7

best for most plants — 6

average garden soils — 5, 4

swamp Peats — 3, 2

ACID — 1, 0

neutral. Almost all vege-
tables will thrive in a
soil with a pH between
6 and 7, which is
slightly acid. If the
test indicates your
soil is acid you will
have to correct this
by the addition of
lime or woodashes.
     The amount of lime
to use will vary
greatly according to the
acidity of the soil.
Generally, clay soils
will need more lime
than sandy soils.
On very acid soils
the need for lime
will be much higher
than for soils which
are slightly acid.

If the test indicates your soil is moderately acid, say with a pH of 5, you can add between fifty and seventy-five pounds of dolomite lime for each one thousand square feet. This would be sufficient for three or four years.

Dolomite lime has magnesium besides calcium, which makes it more useful than ground limestone. Since both are naturally ground rock, either is suitable. In some places it is possible to get ground oyster or clam shells, or ground marble if you live near a quarry.

Lime can be applied any time of the year

with Fall being slightly preferable since there is more time for it to work into the soil. The longer the lime has to work the better it is. Besides, you have more time too.

Lime can be applied with a shovel or by hand. The idea is to whiten the surface and to rake it into the top two inches of the soil.

Lime can also be added to the compost heap.

Liming can have other, indirect benefits because it helps create a condition favorable to the breakdown of organic matter. It helps break up a heavy, tight soil too. Also members of the cabbage family are subject to club root which does not thrive in an alkaline environment.

Wood ashes also help control the cabbage maggot.

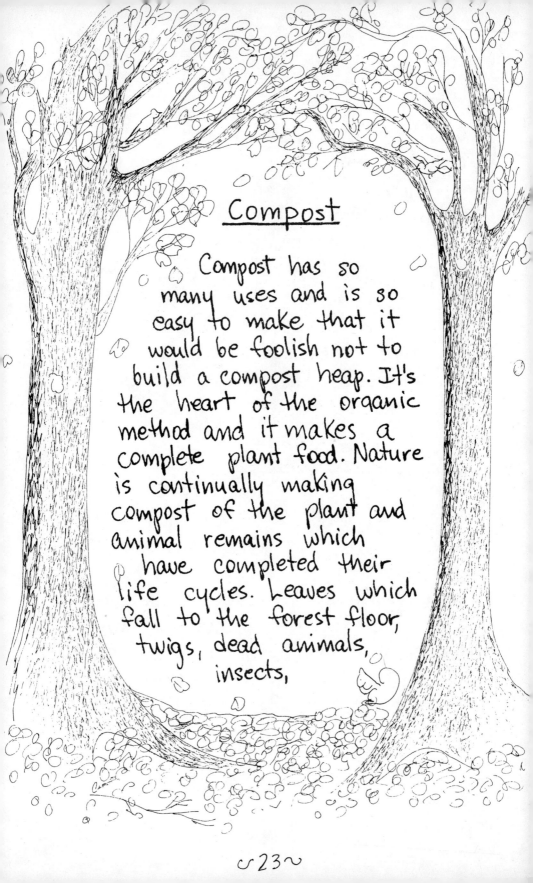

Compost

Compost has so many uses and is so easy to make that it would be foolish not to build a compost heap. It's the heart of the organic method and it makes a complete plant food. Nature is continually making compost of the plant and animal remains which have completed their life cycles. Leaves which fall to the forest floor, twigs, dead animals, insects, all help to replenish and to complete nature's plan.

There are several methods of making compost. Sir Albert Howard, who is often called the "father of organic gardening" devised a method which sped up the fermentation process. His system is called the "Indore Method". Named for a town in India, it is the one we use.

Building a Compost Heap:

First, a rectangle is layed out in a shady spot close to the garden. A box with no top and no bottom is built to sit squarely on the ground. Make it about five feet wide by ten feet long by five feet deep. That would be a good size. It will give you a compost heap of 250 cubic feet which will shrink to approximately half that volume when finished, or about 40 wheel barrow loads. This will be sufficient to put a one inch layer over an entire garden of 1500 square feet.

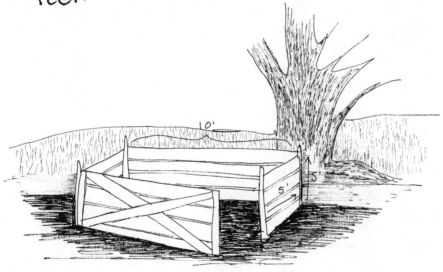

The more varied the materials which go into the pile the better it will be. It so happens your compost heap will even have an international flavor. You will be recycling fertility from around the world, trace minerals in coffee grounds, banana peels, tea leaves, etc. This way a more balanced plant food will result.

We keep a bucket in the kitchen to collect all the vegetable wastes and we add them to the heap. If you do not have a compost pile, kitchen garbage can be buried in trenches between the rows of vegetables. Just dig a hole, put the garbage in and cover with soil. There won't be any odors.

The first six inch layer of the heap consists of vegetable matter — leaves, hay, kitchen garbage, lawn clippings, anything which will decay.

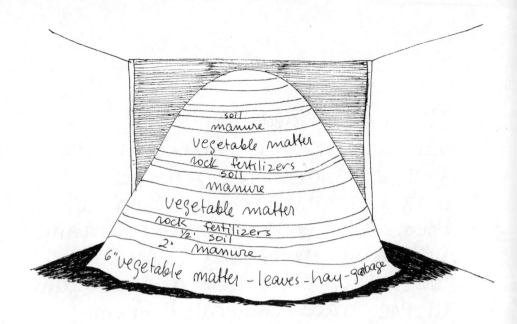

soil
manure
vegetable matter
rock fertilizers
soil
manure
vegetable matter
rock fertilizers
1/2' soil
2" manure
6" vegetable matter - leaves - hay - garbage

Then place a 2 inch layer of
manure on top. Substitutes for the
manure can be blood meal, soy
meal, cotton seed meal, or dried
cow manure. The manure supplies
nitrogen for the bacteria to aide
the decay. On top of these two
layers we place a layer of soil
about a half inch thick. Soil acts
as a yeast. The layering of
materials is repeated until the
pile is five feet high. Usually
the pile is built over a period
of time until it is completed.

It's a good idea to add various rock fertilizers to the pile besides the animal and vegetable refuse. Some of them are rock phosphate, granite dust, and greensand (which comes from the sea and contains all the trace minerals). From here on in the only thing to do is to wait for it to rot. An occasional turning will speed up the process, letting the air in. If it feels dry, water it so that it will have the consistency of a damp sponge. It will be finished in six months to a year.

There is also a way of making compost in 14 days. Shred all materials with a lawn mower or shredder. Turn the pile every 3 days and keep it moist. With this method there is no need to layer the materials.

For a complete discussion of compost heaps we refer you to Rodale's <u>Complete Book of Composting</u> which is <u>the</u> book on compost science.

Finished compost should look dark brown and have a light and fluffy texture. You may still be able to find an occasional egg shell or a piece of orange rind, but at this stage it is perfectly good to use.

We usually plant winter squash around the outside of the compost pile and this works out well for several reasons. The squash vines will cover the pile with its broad leaves

and will provide some necessary
shade. They will also hide the
pile. We came up with a good
harvest of two bushels of
buttercup squash as well!

Finished compost can be
applied when you are preparing
the soil, covering the garden
with a layer one or two inches
thick. When the plants have made
a good growth, we spread a mulch
of compost around each plant.
But it should not be placed
closer than two inches to the
stem of the plant because it
might cause it   to rot. This
even happened
when we placed
some blood
meal too close
to some
pepper plants.

A more economical way of using compost would be to place a two inch covering over the row you are going to plant your seeds in and dig this into the top few inches. We also put a couple of shovelfuls of compost under each transplant when we set out tomato, pepper, and cabbage plants. This really gets them off to a good start!

Manure

If you are just starting a garden, you probably won't have any compost. The best substitute is well-rotted manure. Fresh manure can be applied in the Fall and is the best way to improve a heavy, clay soil. The manure usually decays before Spring so only a slight loss through leaching and decomposition results.

We apply fresh manure on the garden in the Fall after everything is harvested. Next, we rototill the manure into the top few inches of soil, including any mulch which might be left. This will leave the garden in good shape for an early start the next Spring.

Fresh manure should not be used in the Spring at planting time unless first composted or rotted. The urine in fresh manure would prove too strong for the plants, possibly burning them. Also, the soil organisms would use so many nitrates in decomposing the manure that a nitrogen deficiency would temporarily result.

One pound of manure for each square foot of garden area would be a liberal amount. Half of that would give pretty good results, and twice as much should be used for plants grown for their leaves.... spinach, chard, celery, etc. Chicken, sheep, and rabbit manure are highly concentrated and should be used more sparingly. To be safe, apply these to the compost pile first.

Liquid manure, or manure "tea", is useful for giving plants a boost to stimulate growth. The easiest way to make liquid manure is to fill a burlap bag with any kind of manure, fresh or rotted, (a combination of various manures are better than only one kind), place the filled burlap bag in a large container such as a garbage can, and fill it with water. In a few days the "tea" will be ready. But it is too strong to use directly and should be diluted with water until it is the color of weak tea or light amber. This quickly available plant food is especially useful when setting out transplants. Use a cup or two every two weeks, especially if the soil is below average fertility.

If you can't get cow manure a little searching around should reveal a good source of other manure. You might try riding stables, for example, which are usually only too glad to give their manure away free for the hauling. Most garden shops sell dried and composted manures and these are fine too, although they can be prohibitively expensive. But a much smaller quantity is needed, since they are highly concentrated. Even a small quantity is better than none at all.

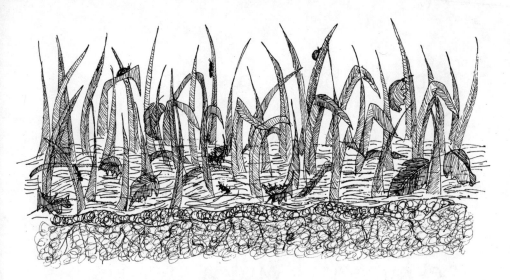

Mulches

Organic gardeners try to follow Nature's example as closely as possible. If you were to search the fields and woods, it would be difficult to find bare, exposed soil except under extreme circumstances. Old Mother Nature always keeps the soil covered and protected. A mulch is a layer of material placed on the

ground both to protect
and enrich the soil, and
to make cultivation
unnecessary.
      Perennial crops like
asparagus, rhubarb, and
raspberries, Kept under a
permanent mulch of hay,
leaves, manure, or sawdust,
are greatly benefitted.
These materials are placed
between the rows and
plants to smother the
weeds, and to feed the
soil at the same time. Our
small planting of blueberry
bushes, for instance, are
mulched with 6 inches of
pine needles and wood
chips. The pine needles
Keep the soil acid, which
is necessary for the
blueberries, and also

Keep the soil loose while holding the moisture in.

We have tried keeping our garden under a permanent hay mulch as suggested by Ruth Stout in her book How To Have a Green Thumb Without An Aching Back. She explains how she uses a permanent year-round mulch over her entire garden. This method eliminates most of the garden chores such as spading, hoeing, weeding, and cultivating. We have tried this for a couple of years with varying degrees of success. Since our soil is a heavy, clay, it dries out very slowly and remains cold in the Spring. A mulch placed on this type of soil too early would only aggravate this condition. (A sandy soil can be kept under a year-round mulch with better results.) We wait for the soil to warm up nicely and the seedlings to be 4-6 inches high before spreading the mulch.

Add to the mulch as needed to keep down the weeds, if they should manage to come through. We use hay that is no longer any good for animal feed, either because it is too old or has been rained on, but it makes an ideal mulch. Layers of hay can be peeled off the bales easily and, when placed

between the rows, make
the garden look attractive.
It usually takes about
25 bales to mulch our
40 x 50 foot garden for the
entire season. At the end
of the year this mulch
will have broken down
quite a bit and only a
thin layer will remain.
This can be left on until
early Spring but should
be raked aside to let
the sun warm the soil.
What we usually do,
however, is to rototill the
mulch under in the Fall
along with any manure
or compost we might have.
          After doing this
for a couple of years,
our soil has become much
richer and lighter

and we might try the year-round mulch system again. Here is a list of materials that makes a good mulch and will also provide humus when incorporated with the soil: hay, straw, sawdust, peat moss, grass clippings, dead weeds, wood chips, pine needles, ground corn cobs, leaf mold, leaves, seaweed, and garbage.

We have also used newspapers and cardboards between the rows and they do a good job in a pinch. Recently, black plastic has come on the market for use as mulching material. The plastic comes in various widths and can be rolled out between the rows. The only objection to this material is that it is non-degradable and does not add any humus to the soil. But black plastic keeps the soil warmer than any organic mulch would. This helps such heat-loving crops as tomatoes, peppers, and eggplants to mature a little earlier than they normally would.

Fertilizers

It is not too difficult for the beginning gardener to distinguish between the natural (organic) and chemical (inorganic) fertilizers. Besides the various manures and composts, natural fertilizers are made of animal products like bone meal, blood meal, hoof & horn meal, vegetable products like soya meal, cottonseed meal, sea weed, and mineral products like rock phosphate, granite meal, greensand, and woodashes.

Of the three most essential plant foods, nitrogen, phosphorus, and potash, the one most often lacking and costly to replace is nitrogen. Since it is so highly soluble, it is readily washed out of the soil in drainage water. Besides the nitrogen in manure and compost, it can be supplied by blood meal (15% N), soya meal (7% N), cottonseed meal (7% N), and fish meal (7-8% N). The last three items are applied at the rate of 50 lbs. to each 1000 sq. ft. of garden area. Blood meal, which is more highly concentrated, is used at half that rate.

Phosphorous causes fruit to ripen earlier, increases root development, and generally helps plants to resist disease. Phosphorous is most effective when there is an adequate supply of humus in the soil. The best and most readily available

source is ground phosphate
rock. Bone meal is another
good source. Apply these
at the rate of 100-150 lbs.
per sq. ft. This should be
sufficient for about 3 years.
     Potash is essential
to the growth of all plants.
Large quantities are used
by the root crops. When a
potash deficiency is present,
plants will be stunted, with
weak stems, and the edges
of the leaves will develop
a yellow color later changing
to brown. This element is best
applied by using the natural
mineral fertilizers such as
granite dust, rock potash, and
greensand. Apply these at the
same rate as rock phosphate.
Wood ashes can be applied
at the rate of 50 lbs. per

1000 sq. ft.

Before applying any fertilizers, it is advisable to find out which elements are lacking and which are not. This will save money and a lot of wasted effort. In general, the natural fertilizers are slow acting and little chance of injury results even if more of an element is applied than needed. This is especially true of the mineral fertilizers such as the various rock powders.

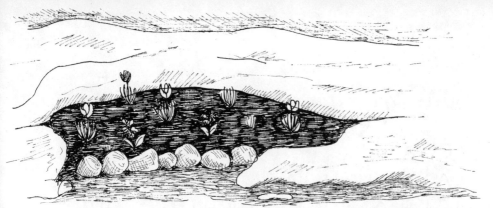

Starting Seeds Early

    In the colder parts of the country the garden season does not start until May. Up here in Northern Vermont the snow doesn't melt until the end of April. The earliest we have been able to plant outside, allowing for the ground to dry, is May 15, and then only the hardiest vegetables.

    With such a short growing season some plants, such as tomatoes and peppers, could not be brought to maturity unless they were started early indoors. If you have a greenhouse you are

most fortunate. The next best
thing we have found are
plant-growing lights. These
are ordinary 4 ft. florescent
fixtures with special bulbs
such as Gro-Lux and
Plant-Gro. (See sources of
supply.)

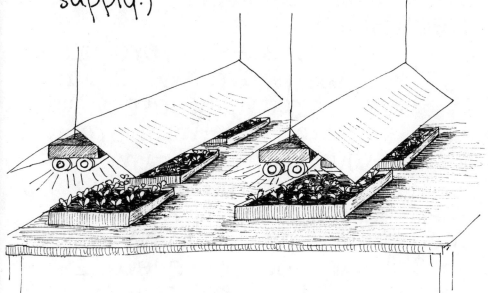

We have used these
special lights for starting
our earliest plants with
wonderful results. We also

use them for raising salad greens all winter. Our three fixture set-up (each fixture contains two 40 watt bulbs) allows us to grow many tomatoes, peppers, celery, cabbage, broccoli, cauliflower, and many flower and herb seedlings.

The seedlings produced in this way are the equal of those grown in greenhouses and superior to those grown on a windowsill. A timer is handy for maintaining the correct day/night cycle. The lights are left on about 16-18 hours out of every 24 hour period, since plants need a rest too. We try to keep the tops of the seedlings about 4 inches from the lights.

Seeds planted under lights also mature earlier than those started on a window sill or in a cold frame. The sun always shines under the lights — there are no cloudy days to hold up growth. We also feed the seedlings with a liquid fish fertilizer every time we water, generally about once a week. We use one teaspoon to a gallon of water and this keeps the seedlings in a state of lusty growth.

Another product we have used with fine results are compressed peat pots sold under the trade names "Jiffy-7's" and "Park's One-Steps". These peat pots are made of sterile peat moss and expand to 7 times their original size when you add water.

Since using these, we haven't had any problems with damping-off which is a fungus disease that attacks the seedlings at the point where they emerge from the soil. This problem is solved by the sterile nature of the peat moss in these pots. There isn't any mixing of the soil. All you do is add water and plant two seeds in each pot. When seedlings are an inch tall we cut off the least promising one with a scissor so as not to disturb the roots of the one remaining.

These pots can be purchased from most of the mail order seed houses. We bought a case of 1000 four years ago since unit prices are much cheaper when bought in large quantities. And since they are compressed into a small wafer, there is no storage problem.

Our garden plan for 1973

Asparagus			
Cucumbers	Peas-double rows - 6" apart		Strawberries
	Peas-double rows - 6" apart		
	Snap beans (green)		
	Snap beans (yellow + purple)		
	Chard / Endive / Escarole		
Summer Squash	Lettuce		Corn
	Spinach (followed by peppers)		
	Beets - wide row		
	Carrots - wide row		
	Onions - wide row		
Winter Squash	Leeks / Salsify / Mustard greens		
	Turnips / Kohlrabi / Parsnips		
	Cabbage seed / Broccoli seed / Cauliflower seed		tomatoes
	Cauliflower plants / Broccoli plants		
	Cabbage plants / Brussel sprouts		

(PATH between left plots and right column)

Our garden plan for 1972
(not drawn to scale)

← 50' →

	Asparagus			
3 ft.	Asparagus			
2½ ft.	Early cabbage plants / Brussel sprout plants		Strawberries	
2½ ft.	Broccoli plants / Cauliflower plants			Winter Squash
2½ ft.	Cabbage seed / Broccoli seed / Cauliflower seed			/ Summer Squash
2 ft.	Turnips / Kohlrabi / Parsnips			/ Cucumbers
2 ft.	Carrots - wide row		Tomatoes	
2 ft.	Beets - wide row			
2 ft.	Onions - wide row			
2 ft.	Lettuce			
2 ft.	Spinach - double row, 6" apart (followed by peppers)			
2 ft.	Swiss Chard / Endive / Celery			
2 ft.	Corn Salad / Escarole / Celtuce / Celeriac		Corn	
2½ ft.	Snap beans (yellow)			
2½ ft.	Snap beans (green)			
2½ ft.	Peas - double rows, 6" apart			
3 ft.	Peas - double rows			

← 35' → ← 15' →

40'

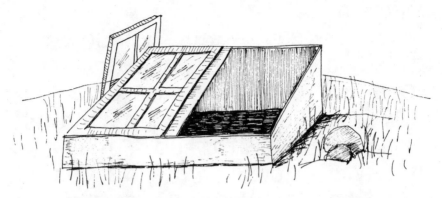

Coldframes and Hotbeds

Coldframes and hotbeds are useful all year long in a cold climate. They provide greenhouse-like conditions and have many uses. Their whole point is to control the environment surrounding the plants. Basically a cold frame is a bottomless box which is placed on the ground and fitted with a removable cover of glass or clear plastic.

Seeds may be sown directly in the coldframe long before the regular garden season begins. Plants that were started earlier in the house can be put in the coldframe to get them used to the weather (hardened-off). Then they can be transplanted to the garden when conditions are more favorable.

By starting plants earlier they can be brought to maturity sooner. This is especially important when trying to grow such heat-loving plants such as melons, peppers, tomatoes, and eggplant. In a cold climate these crops could not be brought to maturity without this early start.

If some source of heat is added to the coldframe its usefulness is increased and it can now be called a hotbed. The heat source can come from either fresh horse (or poultry) manure or from electricity. For a manure-heated hotbed an excavation of 2½ feet is necessary. Then the manure is placed in the hotbed to a depth of 18 inches and topped with 6-8 inches of soil, which should contain about ⅓ compost. The manure must be fresh or it will not give off heat. It should also be wetted down to start fermentation.

Probably, it will be necessary to wait a few days for the temperature in the hotbed to drop down to 80° before you plant. If it is much hotter than that it could kill the seeds. (A thermometer, placed in the hotbed would be helpful.)

Temperature control is more difficult in a manure-heated hotbed than in one heated electrically. Electric heating cables are placed about 6-8 inches below the soil. These heating cables contain a thermostat which maintains a 70° temperature that is ideal for growing all seedlings.

If the hotbed is a standard 3x6 feet, cables

and thermostat will cost about $8.00 total, and can be used for many years. Cost for electricity varies in different locations, but $1.00 per month would be a reasonable estimate. Since a hotbed makes it possible to raise salad greens, kale, and mustard, all winter, I figure we still come out ahead judging from their prices at the store.

The main advantage of an electric hotbed over a manure-heated one is obvious: manure loses its heating ability in a few weeks when fermentation stops. Also, an electric hotbed can be changed to a coldframe by merely

turning off the electricity.
Coldframes are made
the same way as hotbeds
except that an excavation
is unnecessary for a
coldframe. Permanent coldframes can be made of
concrete, cinder blocks, or
2 inch thick boards. Old
storm windows make
excellent sashes for the
cover. Or 4 mil. clear plastic
can be used. Of course,
if you have some extra
storm windows, make the
frame to fit the windows.
Ventillation will be
necessary when the sun is
shining. Even if the outside
temperature is 40°, it can
still go to over 100° inside
the hotbed or coldframe.
Also, water evaporation

occurs rapidly and close attention to the bed will be a daily necessity, no matter how it is heated. In very cold weather it will be necessary to cover the hotbed or coldframe with some kind of additional protection. Old blankets and burlap bags or anything handy will do.

A temporary coldframe can be made easily and quickly by using hay bales.

The bales are placed in a sunny spot and layed out to form a rectangle. Fit a cover of glass or plastic on the top. This frame is especially useful for hardening-off seedlings that were started earlier in the house. After this coldframe is no longer useful, the hay makes excellent mulch.

spade

spading fork

trowel

roto-tiller

Preparing the Soil

Basically there are three ways of preparing the soil. You can spade it by hand. You can plow and harrow it. Or you can roto-till it. Having tried all three methods, we found that rototilling does the best job.

If yours is a new garden site, the planting area should be staked out and all trash, brush, and stones removed. If there is a tall growth of weeds, first cut them up with a lawn mower before preparing the soil.

Fall is a good time to start a future garden site. The sods will have a chance to rot during the Winter and, by Spring, will add humus to the soil. Don't try to prepare a soil that is too wet. It should form a ball that easily breaks apart when squeezed. Sandy soils can be prepared earlier than clay soils since they dry out quicker.

When rototilling new sod it usually requires 3 or 4 passes, going an inch or two deeper with each pass.

But whatever method is used,
the soil should be worked
to a depth of at least 8 inches.
On the first pass use the
rototiller in low gear at the
slowest possible speed.
	After the sods are
broken up, spread manure or
compost, and work it into the
soil. In fact, any time you till
the garden is a time to
fertilize the soil. All that is
left to do in Spring is to
rake smooth the area and
the garden is ready for
planting seeds.

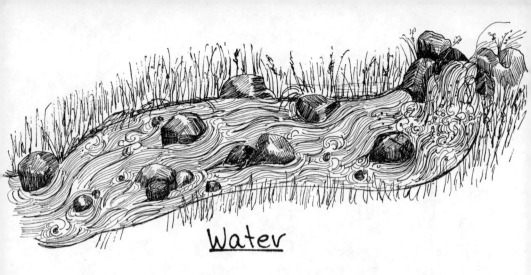

<u>Water</u>

Water is the cheapest fertilizer for your garden. This point is often neglected since no one makes money selling water. Without water, plant growth could not exist at all. The most important consideration for growing succulent vegetables is <u>never ever</u> let the plants dry out and wilt. One thorough watering is much better than frequent light sprinkles because deep watering encourages root growth.

It might be necessary to irrigate during some part

of the season, usually during July and August when rainfall is sometimes inadequate. The soil should be kept moist but not so waterlogged that air cannot enter. Organic matter in the soil holds the water for use as plants need it. Without organic matter, water passes through the soil too quickly and carries plant nutrients along with it.

Cultivating & Weeding

Undoubtedly, mulching is the best way to control weeds and to keep the soil cool and moist. If a mulch is not available or if you prefer not to follow this practice, another method of weed control will have to be used. In that case the best tool for weeding in a small garden is the common hoe.

Weeds must be kept under control since they rob crops of water, light, and plant food. Most weeds grow much faster than cultivated crops so the best time to kill them is when they first come up. Annual weeds are easy to control, but deep-rooted plants or those with underground stems are a little harder to handle. Frequent hoeing will keep even these from growing, eventually starving the underground parts.

Hoeing also keeps the soil loose and aerated, allowing the roots to grow more easily. Cultivating creates a dust mulch which slows down evaporation, thereby keeping more moisture

in the soil for the plant.
Keep the hoe sharp and
you will save lots of time
for more important chores.
Don't hoe too deeply or too
close to plants, whose roots
or stems might be injured.
Some hand weeding will be
necessary close to the plants.

Insect & Disease Control

Plants grown in good, humusy soil are considerably less subject to insect attack and disease. Bacteria and fungi, which naturally abound in organic matter, secrete substances much like antibiotics, controlling and more often destroying disease organisms.

As already mentioned, no garden should be completely free of insects. This poor creature might be the gardener's friend and ally, or even if he is the "enemy" this insect has a purpose. Why is he there? One reason is to destroy an unhealthy plant. Nature is telling you this plant is not fit to eat. This insect is just doing his job, as Nature intended.

By now everyone is familiar with the ecological havoc caused by DDT, aldrin, dieldrin, and a host of other chemical insecticides. Not only the large-scale farmers, but also the backyard gardeners have begun to realize the urgent necessity

of banning these deadly
poisons. Most states have
already banned the use of
DDT, but this is far from
a victory. The newer chemicals
are even more toxic!

In all the years we
have been gardening, we
have never found it
necessary to spray any
vegetables. This does not mean
that insects have not
threatened our crops, but we
took simple control measures
at the right time and
little damage resulted.
Next to having a healthy soil,
We encourage Nature's best
insecticides: birds. Many times
while taking an early
morning walk through the
garden, we have noticed
swallows and fly catchers

flying up and down the vegetable rows, searching under, over, and around the plants, devouring every insect they could find.

To control slugs and cutworms, who do most of their damage at night, we encourage toads who also feed at night. In Europe, toads are sold at the market place for just this purpose. In early spring, after the young toads have hatched, we collect all we can find. We place shallow dishes of water in various shady places about the garden to encourage them to stay.

There are also a number of beneficial insects that the gardener can encourage. Lady bugs,

praying mantises, and green
lacewings can be established
around the garden.

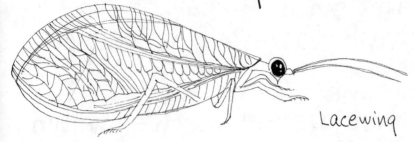

Lacewing

They can be collected or
purchased and brought in.

Certain herbs have
insect repellant properties.
Some of the best to include,
planted among the vegetables,
are tansy, rue, mints,
pyrethrum daisy, marigolds,
nastertiums, savory, thyme,
garlic, and onions.
Another point to
consider is yearly rotation
of vegetables. Try not to

plant the same vegetables or a close relative in the same place each year. Also, try to plant disease resistant varieties whenever possible.

One of the most primitive, yet effective, methods of controling insects is handpicking. Many kinds of caterpillars and insect eggs can be eliminated by this method.

When all else fails and a serious attack is imminent, the gardener can now turn to the safe botanical insecticides: Rotenone and Pyrethrum. Check the label to make sure nothing else has been added. These two insecticides are harmless to man and animals and are derived from natural substances found in plants. For a more complete discussion I highly recommend <u>Gardening Without Poisons</u> by Beatrice Trim Hunter.

Jerusalem Artichoke

The Jerusalem Artichoke (helianthus tuberosus) is not an artichoke nor from Jerusalem. The name "Jerusalem" is probably a corruption of the Italian word "girasole" or the Spanish "girasol" meaning sunflower. It is a perennial sunflower native to North America and bears oblong tubers much like the potato. The early settlers learned to cultivate the plant from the Indians and was later brought back to Europe.

The plant grows 5 to 10 feet tall with 2-3 inch yellow flowers. You might have seen them growing wild around roadways, farmhouses, and fields since they have long ago escaped cultivation.

The tubers look like knobby medium-sized potatoes and have a sweet, nutty flavor similar to Chinese water chestnuts. Unlike the potato it doesn't contain any starch, and sugar is stored in the form of levulose, making it excellent for diabetics.

They can be grown in all parts of the coutry as long as rainfall is sufficient. Very hardy, they will grow in all kinds of soils that are reasonably well drained.

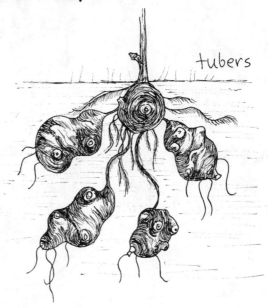

tubers

It does well on land considered too poor for even the potato. But the better the soil the larger the tubers and yield.

They should be grown in an area all to themselves away from the garden because they soon spread and completely take over an area. Little cultivation is needed because the plants are so vigorous they will soon choke out weeds.

Planting may be done in the fall or in early spring. Whole tubers are planted about four inches deep and two feet apart in rows three feet apart.

Harvesting

After the first killing frost in September or

October the large woody tops of the plants are cut off and left for mulch. The tubers grow in a wide area under each plant but careful digging should reveal all the tubers you can possibly eat.

The tubers have almost no skin, unlike the potato and are easily injured. They won't keep very long in storage so only a few weeks supply should be dug at one time. They need moisture and cool temperatures for storage and keep best just left in the ground.

They can be gathered anytime in the fall and Winter when the ground is unfrozen, and again in the Spring. Any undug tubers will sprout in the Spring and perpetuate the planting. Once the initial planting is done, you can enjoy them year after year without any work except harvesting (which is more like a treasure hunt any way).

No distinct varieties have been developed.

Cooking

Since the tubers are starchless they won't taste mealy like potatoes but they can be used in any potato recipe. They are especially tasty sliced raw into a salad, having a sweet, crunchiness all their own. Or rub the tubers with oil and bake in the oven as you would a potato. Try adding them to Chinese dishes during the last minute of cooking.

If you don't find
any growing wild or in
a friend's garden, tubers
can be ordered from:
Burgess Seed & Plant Co.,
Galesburg, Michigan 49053.

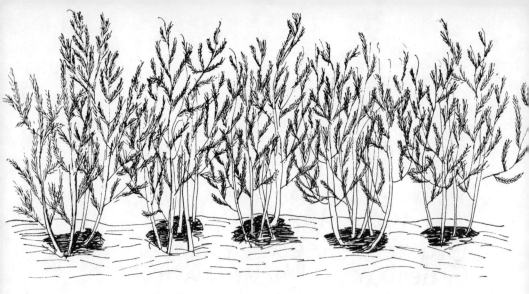

<u>Asparagus</u>

Asparagus is a perennial vegetable, which means it returns every year from the same root. It should be planted at one side of the garden so it won't interfere with the usual garden operations.

Aside from being a delicious, healthful vegetable, it comes along before any of the regular garden vegetables are ready. After picking wild dandelions from the fields for the earliest greens, the

Asparagus season is just getting started. How nice to have these two vegetables so early without any work, and no chance of failure!

Once planted, an asparagus bed, with little care, will last indefinitely. Asparagus will grow on almost any kind of soil that is well drained. It is completely hardy even in the coldest parts of the country. In fact, it doesn't grow as well in the southern climates.

The soil for asparagus should be thoroughly prepared since it will occupy the land for many years. After planting there can be no further preparation. The soil should be made as rich as possible with manure and compost and a generous amount of lime mixed in, if needed. The old practice of deep planting has been found to be unnecessary and not even beneficial. That's certainly good news since the idea of digging a four-foot-deep trench doesn't appeal to many people.

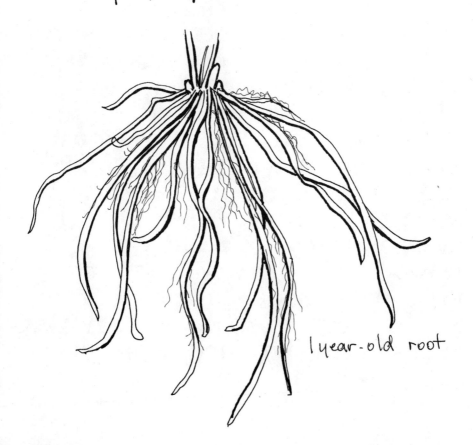

1 year-old root

Asparagus can be grown from seed, but it is much easier to plant one-year-old roots which can be purchased inexpensively from any seed house. This saves a year and you can have it that much sooner. Twenty-five roots are usually the minimum sold and will provide enough for a small family — but not enough for freezing. Fifty roots will give almost one meal a day for a month and a half and some for freezing too. Asparagus freezes so well that it is very difficult to tell the fresh from the home-frozen product. Home-grown asparagus is tastier than the kind you buy at the store and should be eaten as soon after picking as possible. Try it raw!

You can expect to harvest about a pound of asparagus from each plant after the third year. I checked the price of frozen asparagus at the store and found that a 10 oz. package cost 79¢. At those prices I figure that our bed of 50 plants saves us quite a bit. No stalks should be harvested the year they are planted and they should be left alone the second year also. This 2 year wait accounts for the high price of asparagus.

Planting is done in the early Spring as soon as the soil is dry enough to work. Dig a trench about

4 to 6 inches deep and a
foot wide. Place the roots
about 18 inches apart in
the row and keep the
rows 3 feet apart. Cover

asparagus
trenches

the roots with only 2 inches
of soil — any deeper might
smother the stalks. As the
plants grow, more soil is
added until the trench is
filled in completely. It is
easiest to maintain a bed

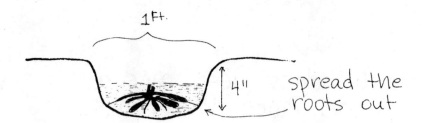

1 Ft.

4" spread the roots out

that is kept under a constant mulch, eliminating the need for all weeding and cultivation. Hay, sawdust, woodchips, and especially compost and manure, are good mulches. Asparagus roots go down very deep once established and watering will not be needed.

The space between the asparagus rows need not be wasted! A small, low-growing crop like lettuce can be planted there and will benefit from the slight shade.

Varieties

Most of the varieties sold are of the Washington strains, Mary & Martha. These were developed when Asparagus Rust threatened the entire asparagus industry. This disease is eliminated by planting the rust-resistant varieties. Recently, a new hybrid has appeared called 'Faribo Hybrid.' It is sold by Farmer Seed & Nursery!

Harvesting

Asparagus is ready to harvest when the stalks are six to eight inches high. They can usually be cut clean for 6 to 8 weeks.

Perhaps the easiest way to harvest asparagus is merely to break off the stalks which are ready. This method has several advantages. It doesn't injure new shoots coming up as might happen with a knife. By breaking them you include only the tender, edible parts.

You can tell when to stop harvesting by the size of the stalks. Once skinny stalks begin to appear they should be left alone for the rest of the season to insure a good crop for the following year.

The best way to cook asparagus is to steam them in about an inch of water. Stand them vertically in a small but high pot, like a coffee pot, with the tips at the top — and steam until tender. This insures the greatest amount of vitamin retention. Then you can do whatever else you wish with them.

Fresh home-grown asparagus are sweet and delicious when raw and cut up into a salad.

Beans

String beans, which are now 'stringless' as a result of selective breeding, are more correctly called snap beans or bush beans. Beans are warm season plants and are planted after danger of frost has passed. In our part of northern Vermont planting usually begins about June 1st for the heat-loving crops. We often take a chance and plant a week to 10 days earlier since there is nothing to lose but a few seeds.

Beans are capable of utilizing atmospheric nitrogen with the help of bacteria which are found in the nodules on the roots of the plants. This feature makes beans a very desirable addition to your garden. Instead of taking nitrogen they add it to the soil and enrich it. Peas also belong to the same family (leguminosea) but their culture is different.

Snap beans

Snap beans are easy to grow, even the beginner

is sure of success. This makes them, a good item for a child's garden. Beans are available in many kinds, to suit personal preference: green bean, yellow-podded (also called wax beans), purple-podded, shell beans, pole beans, and lima beans.

Beans have a reputation of doing well in poor soil, but the richer the soil, the better the crop will be. They are also heavy yielders, averaging about a pound for each foot of row planted. Using this information and the available space it is easy for you to compute the amount to plant.

When planting beans it is usually a good idea to soak the seeds overnight

in warm water. This speeds
up germination, especially if
the soil is on the dry side.
Just before planting coat the
seed with a nitrogen-fixing
bacteria such as Legume
Aid. Sprinkle it on with a
spoon of pancake or corn
syrup or something gooey.
This will give you a better
crop and will help to add
nitrogen to the soil, especially
if other legumes have not
been grown there before.
This bacteria is perfectly safe
to handle.
        Place the seeds with
the eyes down 2 inches apart
in the row and cover with
one inch of loose soil — or
better still, with one inch
of fine compost or leaf mold.
This will prevent compaction

and a crust from forming, making it easier for the seedlings to come up. Keep the rows 18 inches apart. When the plants are six inches tall, spread a mulch between the rows. All varieties mature in 7 to 8 weeks.

Varieties

Green-podded: Tender-crop, Tenderette, Greencrop, Burpee's Tenderpod, Topcrop.

Yellow-podded: Eastern Butterwax has the best flavor of all the wax beans we have tried. Other good varieties are Kinghorn Wax, Pencil Pod Wax, and Burpee's Brittle Wax.

Purple-podded: Royalty.

This variety turns green after cooking 2 minutes in boiling water, providing a built-in blanching indicator for home freezing. It also grows in colder soil than other kinds. Picking is easier with this variety because of the contrast between the green foliage and the purple pods. Excellent quality.

Harvesting

To get the best flavor and texture, pods should be harvested before they are fully grown and while the seeds are small. They will become tough and stringy if left too long on the plants. If they are picked regularly,

they will put forth new pods
for several weeks more.
Stay out of the bean patch
when the plants are wet
to control the spread of
fungus diseases.

Pole Beans

Some kind of support is needed for these climbing beans. They can sometimes reach a height of ten feet in a season. Wooden poles 8 feet long (with the bark left) on are ideal for this purpose. I usually cut them in the early Spring when there is not much else to do in the garden. They can be placed 3 feet apart and sunk in the ground individually, or three poles can be tied together at the top to form a teepee.

Five or six seeds are planted around each pole, keeping the seeds a few inches apart. After the plants are up and growing, thin them out so that only three or four of the best plants remain to each pole. If they are picked often, they will produce until killed by frost.

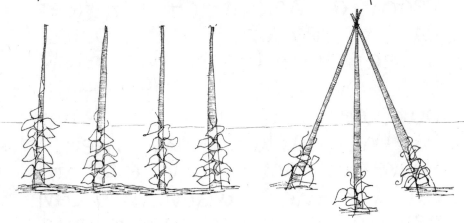

If you find yourself with too many beans let them fully mature. These can be left to dry in the pods and they will be excellent to use during the winter for baked beans.

Good varieties we have tried are: Kentucky Wonder,

Romana (which are the so-called 'Italian green beans'), and Burpee's Golden Pole Bean.

Lima Beans + Soy Beans

We have tried growing these for a number of years but they just refuse to mature in a northern climate. They need much more heat than snap beans and a longer growing season. At least 10 weeks are needed in the southern part of the country and a few additional weeks in the north to mature a crop. For those who want to try them, their culture is the same as snap beans. Good luck!

<u>Beets</u>

Beets thrive best in a cool season and can be grown for a Spring, Summer, or Fall crop in the North. In the South they are grown during the Winter. They are hardy and can be planted as soon as the soil is workable in the Spring. Successive plantings should be made to supply young tender beets through-out the season and some for winter storing, if desired.

Beets can be grown on any good garden soil, but thrive best in a moist well-drained loam. The soil should be thoroughly and deeply prepared, and then raked smooth. Beets do not do well in an acid soil. In fact, beets are often used as an indicator of soil acidity. The PH should be between 6 and 7. If lower than PH 6, lime should be added in a one inch layer over the bed, then dug in.

We plant beets in slightly raised, short beds

instead of rows and we
get four times as many
beets as we might otherwise
get in the same amount
of space.

First, we rake
smooth an
area 14 inches
wide by 10 feet
long and plant
4 rows side
by side,
spaced 4 inches
apart. Seeds are also planted
4 inches apart within the
rows. This gives four 10 foot
long rows — or the equivalent
of one 40 foot long row
in only a 10 foot length
of space. Some hand weeding
and thinning will be
necessary until the plants
grow tall enough. They will

then shade the earth
by themselves and suppress
weed growth.

Each beet seed is
actually a fruit which
contains 2 to 6 seeds and
it is possible to get more
than 100% germination. The
plants come up in clumps
and all but one plant should
be removed so that only
one remains every 4 inches.
So, thinning will always
be necessary and care should
be taken not to disturb the
ones remaining. It is helpful
to soak the seeds overnight

before planting since the
beet seed is hard and
you want to soften it.
This will speed germination.

Varieties

The most popular early kinds are Early Wonder, 55 days to maturity, Crosby's Egyptian, 56 days, and Detroit Dark Red, 65 days, which is the most popular for a late canning beet. For winter storage there is none better than Long Season or "Winter Keeper". These grow very large yet remain sweet and tender no matter how big they get, maturing in 80 days.

A new beet worth trying, Burpee's Golden Beet, is a bright golden color which does not "bleed" like red beets do.

Harvesting

Early beets are tastiest when 1½ to 2 inches around. Don't throw away the tops when harvesting as these make fine greens, either raw in salads or cooked. Young beets should be cooked whole with the skins left on. Leave ½ inch of stem to prevent bleeding. Beets are also good baked whole until tender. Small beets can be canned whole, or pickled. To freeze beets boil or bake till tender, cool and freeze.

Late - planted beets can be stored in a cold damp cellar all winter if the temperature is about

freezing but below 40°.
Harvest before very cold
weather, leaving one inch
of stem attached, and
store in moist sand.

Broccoli

Broccoli has become increasingly popular in recent years. More home gardeners are realizing that it is a good source of vitamins and easy to grow. Broccoli is high in Vitamin A and C with considerable quantities of B Vitamins plus calcium and iron.

For an early crop seeds can be started six weeks before outdoor planting time. Seeds can be started in the house in a sunny window or in a hotbed or somewhat later in a coldframe. The plants are set out when danger of hard freezing is over. It requires 100 days from seed sowing until heading. The plants will then produce a continuous supply of side shoots after the main head is harvested.

The soil for broccoli should be rich, moist, and well-drained with a good supply of lime. It does extremely well in the cooler parts of the country.

Plants are spaced 2 feet apart in rows 2 to 3 feet apart. When setting out young plants, dig out 2 shovelfuls of earth and replace it with compost or rotted manure. Set the plants, and water thoroughly. Cultivate shallowly with the hoe or spread a mulch to conserve water and to eliminate weeding.

For later crops, seeds can be planted directly in the garden. Plant a few seeds every 2 feet. Thin out, leaving only one plant. The extras can be transplanted to form additional rows.

Varieties

Green Comet is a new Japanese hybrid, 55 days to maturity from plant setting. It won the Gold Medal award at the All-America trials. We have grown it for several seasons and found it very vigorous. It matures its large central head very early. This is followed by many side shoots until frost.

Other good varieties include Spartan Early, 55 days, and Waltham 29, 75 days, and Calabrese, 85 days.

Harvesting

The main head should be cut off with a few inches

of stem. Do this before any of the buds show their yellow color. After these are cut, side shoots will appear and these will provide a continuous harvest.
Broccoli is better preserved by freezing than canning.

Insect Control:

Cabbage worms are very fond of all the members of the cabbage family. These are green caterpillars about one inch long and feed on the leaves of the plants. They hatch into the common white butterflies you might have noticed flying around the garden. Birds are very fond of these caterpillars and should take care of this problem. Otherwise it will be necessary to look over the plants and to pick off the caterpillars into a small

can of Kerosene which
will Kill them.
      Another pest sometimes
present is the nasty root
maggot. It feeds on the roots
and causes the plants to
wilt as if they needed
water. Watering the plants
won't help. Wood ashes should
be sprinkled on the ground
besides the plants and
cause the root maggot to
depart.
Recipe: We enjoy broccoli
picked fresh and stir fried
in a wok with a fare
amount of olive oil. Make
sure each piece gets
coated with oil. Add some
sesame seeds and salt or
soy sauce. Stir and cover.
Steam under low heat till
tender, stirring occasionally.

Brussels Sprouts

Brussels sprouts originated in Belgium and is named, as you might expect, after the capital of that country where it has been cultivated for several hundred years. It is a member of the cabbage family. They were developed from the original wild cabbage as were broccoli, cauliflower, collards, kale, and Kohlrabi. The sprouts look like miniature cabbages, in fact, young plants as well as seeds of the cabbage family all look alike.

It takes about four months from seed to maturity. Seeds are usually started inside, 4 to 6 weeks before outside planting time. Or they can be planted directly in the garden — but harvest will be later. A dozen or so plants will be sufficient for most families.

The plants grow two to three feet tall and at maturity look rather unusual to those who have never seen them before. The best way I know to describe them is to say they look like a broomstick with little green golf balls growing on them. They are slow growers and need lots of water and a rich soil.

Brussels sprouts are hardy and they do well in the cooler parts of the country. Frost does not bother them, it actually improves their flavor.

Young plants should be set out early in June and will produce as the fall days become cooler.

Space them 2 feet apart in the row with rows 3 feet apart. Their culture is very similar to broccoli.

As the sprouts first form at the bottom of the plant lower leaves should be broken off. This allows the sprouts room to develop. Continue to remove leaves as they develop until the entire stem is covered with sprouts. When the lower sprouts start developing we also pinch off the top inch or two of the plant. This causes the sprouts to mature quicker by stopping the plant's upward growth — forcing sprouts to grow larger. One plant will usually produce about one hundred sprouts.

Varieties

Older varieties such as Long Island and Catskill have been replaced by a superior Japanese hybrid called Jade Cross. This variety produces twice as many sprouts as the others and has made this vegetable easy and fun to grow. Maturity from plant setting, 90 days.

Harvesting

Lower sprouts are harvested first— before they start to turn yellow. They are simply broken off the plant as needed for the kitchen. They can be harvested over a period of 6-8 weeks and they can be frozen.

In areas where snow comes early the entire plant can be moved from the garden to a cool cellar with moist soil placed around the roots. In this way fresh sprouts can be enjoyed past New Year. In milder areas the plants can be left in the garden all winter, harvesting them as needed.

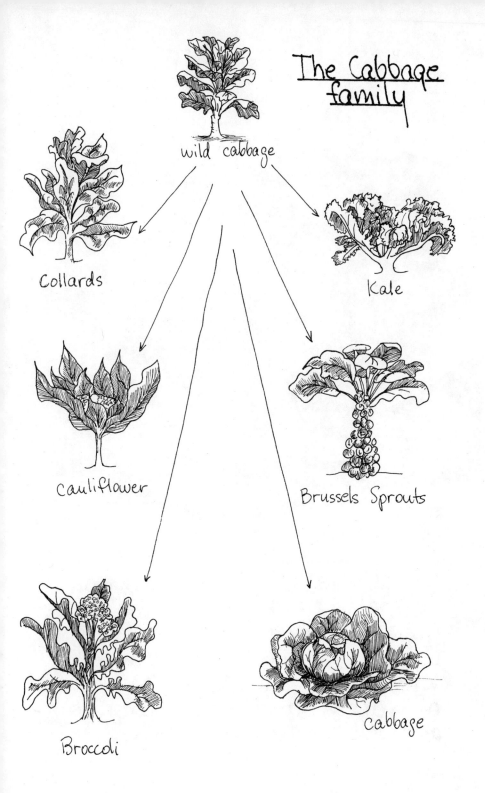

The Cabbage family

wild cabbage

Collards

Kale

Cauliflower

Brussels Sprouts

Broccoli

Cabbage

Cabbage

Cabbage is an easily grown vegetable and one of the highest yielders for the space they occupy. No garden is complete without at least a few heads of green and red varieties, as well as the delicious-tasting savoys.

They can be served in so many ways — boiled, baked, sautéed, or made into sauer- kraut and cole slaw. They are especially valuable in our diet during the winter when salad greens are scarce.

They are grown the same way as their cousins, broccoli, Brussels sprouts, and cauliflower. But their culture is easier. They are not fussy about the weather, being able to stand temperature of 10-15 degrees below freezing.

When possible, plan on having 2 crops — an early summer harvest from plants started early inside, and a fall harvest for storing for winter use.

For the earliest crops, seeds are planted indoors in "flats" or pots at the same time as broccoli. Plants will be large enough to set out in 4 or 5 weeks, or if only a few plants are wanted, you can get them from any nursery or greenhouse. For the late crop, seeds are planted in the garden. By using mid-season varieties, they will mature in early Fall.

Varieties

Perhaps no other vegetable offers such a choice of varieties. There are round headed, conical headed, flat headed, as well as green, red, and savoy. To make the choice even larger, there are early maturing, midseason, and late varieties. Select hybrid varieties whenever possible. They grow more vigorously, are better yielders, and most are resistant to disease. Seed catalogs will

usually tell you if the variety
is a hybrid.
 Early varieties mature
60-70 days from plant setting.
Some of them are Golden
Acre, Early Jersey Wakefield,
Stonehead Hybrid, Emerald
Cross Hybrid. Mid-season and
late varieties mature in
70-90 days. Among them are
Market Prize, Danish
Ballhead, Flat Dutch, and
Burpee's Surehead.
 Red varieties include
Ruby Ball Hybrid, 68 days,
Red Acre, 76 days; and Mamoth
Red Rock, 100 days.
 Savoy varieties are
perhaps the best-tasting of
all the cabbages. Seldom
seen at the market because
they are not considered

good shippers, they are a
flavor treat for home
gardeners. The best of the
savoys are Savoy King Hybrid,
90 days; Vanguard, 68 days,
and Chiefton Savoy, 88 days.

Harvesting

By using different varieties
at the same time you can
get a succession of harvested
cabbages throughout the
seasons.

Cabbages are ready to
harvest when the head feels
firm. An overmature head
will burst or split apart and
will be less useable. To
prevent this, some of the
feeder roots can be cut off
by running a knife in the

soil a couple of inches away from the plant, or by pulling the plant slightly until you feel some of the roots breaking. This will slow down the growth. This is done, of course, when the head is already mature but you still want to leave it in the garden.

Storage

Perhaps the easiest way is to pull the entire plant up— leaves, roots and all. Place the roots in a box of moist soil in a cool place. Or the heads can be stored in plastic bags to help prevent dehydration.

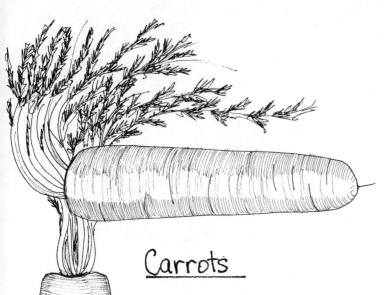

Carrots

Carrots can be easily grown anywhere in the country. They are hardy and can be planted in the early Spring as soon as the soil is dry enough to work. Like beets and other root crops, they are grown from seed planted directly in the garden and mature in 60-80 days depending on the variety. We plant carrots in beds instead of rows, the same way as beets. Seeds can be planted in these beds by simply broadcasting (scattering) the seeds over the area and covering with ½ inch of loose soil.

You might find it helpful to mix some dry sand with the seeds because the carrot seed is small and it is hard to get an even distribution. It is also helpful to mix a few radish seeds with the carrots when planting. Carrot seeds germinate very slowly but the radish, which grows quickly, will mark the area. They also help break any crust which might form on the soil.

When carrot seedlings

are 2-3 inches high they
should be thinned to an
inch apart in all directions.
By this time the radishes
will be ready to eat.
Thinning is best done when
the soil is damp so as not
to disturb the remaining
carrots. When the carrots
start to develop an orange
color they should be thinned
again to two inches apart.
These thinnings are useful
in the kitchen and have a
sweetness which cannot

compare with older, mature roots.

It is a good idea to make another planting at this time to provide young, tender carrots for the Fall and some for storage.

The carrot, like the beet, does best in a deeply worked soil. They do not grow well in a soil that is highly acid. Fresh manure should not be used as it will cause the roots to branch out in deformed shapes. Rotted manure is best applied in the Fall before planting so that it will be broken down by Spring.

Varieties:

Carrots come in all shapes and sizes. The shorter,

stockier types are better
for heavy clay types of soil.
The longer kinds do better
in light, loose, deeply worked
soil. Try both kinds and see
which does better for you.

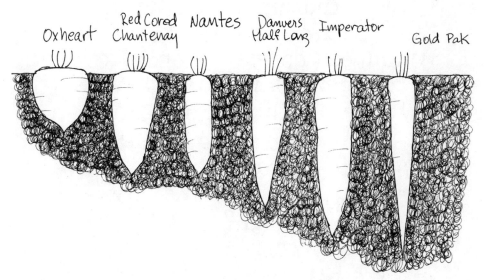

Oxheart   Red Cored   Nantes   Danvers   Imperator   Gold Pak
           Chantenay   Half Long

Oxheart: 4 inches long. Red Cored
Chantenay: 5 inches. Nantes
Half Long: 6 inches. Danvers: 7
inches. Gold Pak and Imperator:
8-9 inches. All of them mature
in approximately the same time.

Harvesting

Carrots can be harvested as soon as they take on their orange color or about ½ inch diameter at the top. This should be part of the thinning process! Carrots can be frozen but late carrots will keep all winter, stored in sand in a cold cellar or unheated garage with high humidity. Cut off the tops but leave a half inch of stem.

Carrots can also be left unharvested in the ground all winter and will keep even better than those stored inside. They will need some protection if snow does not come early, and should be covered with hay. It's a nice treat to dig fresh carrots from the still half-frozen earth in the early Spring.

Cauliflower

Cauliflower does best in a cool, moist climate. It is considered a tricky vegetable to grow. A lot depends on the skill of the gardener but, more importantly, on the weather. A few hot, dry days can cause the plants to form tiny "button heads" which will never grow any larger, ruining your hard work.

Space the plants 2 feet apart within the rows and place the rows 3 feet apart. Rich soil that is well-drained will produce a good crop. Well-rotted manure or compost is almost essential, as well as large quantities of lime. It's hardly possible to make the soil too rich for them. Mulching the plants will help keep the moisture in and the soil cooler during hot weather. If the soil seems dry it will be necessary to water the plants, especially when the heads are forming.

It won't withstand as low a temperature nor as much heat as cabbage. But if weather conditions are right even the novice will succeed.

Cauliflower plants are grown in much the same way as broccoli. Seeds for an early crop are started inside about two weeks later than broccoli and are set out in the garden around June 1st. However, cauliflower is usually more successful as a fall crop. Seeds can be planted directly in the garden anytime until the beginning of July and should produce by September.

Blanching

To get a perfectly pure white head of cauliflower you will need to exclude the sunlight. When the head is small (about the size of an egg) the outer leaves should be brought up over the head and tied loosely at the top. Tie them in a way that still allows the head room to develop. We usually use differently colored wool or string to tie the plants so when cutting it is easy for us to select those which have been tied the longest.

The length of time needed to blanch the head depends on the weather too. In hot weather the heads will usually be blanched in 4 or 5 days. But in cool weather it may take up to 2 weeks.

Varieties

Snow King Hybrid is a good choice for an extra-early harvest. It matures in 50 days after setting out plants.

Snowball Y, 68 days to maturity from plant setting, is good for a late crop. Heads of this variety mature over a long period which can be an advantage to the home gardener.

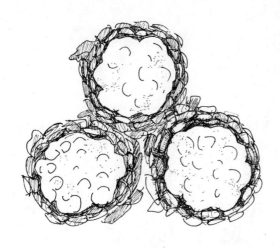

Early Purple-Head and Royal Purple, 85 days to maturity. These two delicious vegetables are never found at the store because they are not solid enough for shipping. They are easier to grow than white cauliflower because they are not blanched. Heads are purple but turn green when cooked.

Harvesting

If left too long the heads will become "riced" and possibly rot. Once a head is ready it won't grow any larger but will deteriorate so it should be harvested promptly. In harvesting, the plant is cut off a few inches below the head with a few leaves attached. Heads will keep in the refrigerator for a few weeks if necessary.

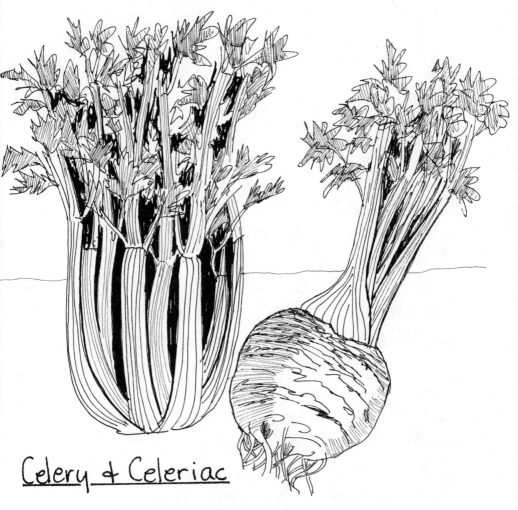

Celery & Celeriac

Celery and Celeriac were both developed from the wild celery, a plant found in marshy places. They are members of the carrot family (Umbelliferae).

Celery

Growing good celery is not too difficult and well worth the effort. But few home gardeners attempt it. The entire plant is edible — leaves and stalks, as well as the roots. Celery does best when the weather is cool with well-distributed rainfall during the growing season. The best soil for celery is one which holds large amounts of water. Humus material should be worked into the area where the plants are to be.

Compost, manure, leaf mold, or peat moss, should be used very generously since celery is a heavy feeder and a poor forager with a small root system.

Celery is a slow grower and plants can be started early inside allowing 10 weeks to raise them before putting out in the garden. Equal parts of soil, peat moss, and sand, are good for starting seeds. Cover the seeds very lightly with a thin sprinkling of sand. Seeds are slow to germinate and must be kept warm and moist. Grow the plants at warm temperatures to prevent premature seeding in the garden later on.

When the plants are 4" tall, or thereabout, they are ready to set out. Allow 8-10 inches between plants and at least two feet between rows.

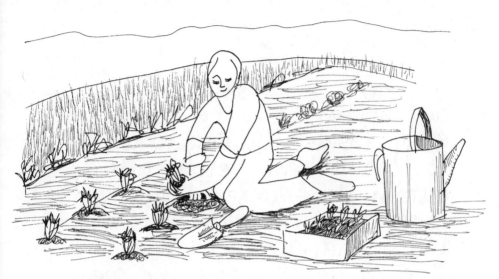

(Celery plants are usually
easy to obtain and many
gardeners prefer to buy them
at the greenhouse.) Or seeds
can be planted directly in
the garden and will mature
somewhat later— in about
4 months. But it isn't
necessary to wait until then
to start harvesting. Stalks
and leaves can be used
when only half grown, until
fully mature.

Celery is sometimes blanched (whitened) to make it less bitter. But many people prefer it green and unblanched. It is hardly necessary though, and unblanched celery is healthier. To blanch, you must exclude light from the stalks so they will turn crisp and yellow. Do this by putting boards, or soil, or paper, around the stalks, but allow the leaves to extend above. Blanching should be complete in 2 or 3 weeks, depending on the weather.

blanching celery with boards or with soil

Varieties

Pascal, Utah 52-70, Golden Self Blanching (no, it doesn't blanch itself), and Tendercrisp, all mature in about 16 weeks.

Storing

Celery can be stored in a cool place for a short while. Dig up the entire plant, roots and all, and place in boxes with moist soil around the roots.

Celeriac

Sometimes called knob or turnip rooted celery, it is grown for its large root which forms slightly above ground and has a flavor like celery. Not often found in gardens nor at the store, it deserves to be better known. It is more popular in Europe and seldom seen here. It is valuable for flavoring soups, stews, grated raw in salads, and can be served as a cooked vegetable. Leaves and stalks are too bitter to be eaten but the root, which grows 2-4 inches in diameter, is mild with a sweet celery taste. Easily grown, the

plants are cared for
exactly like celery, except
that it is not blanched.
The roots can be stored
for winter use the same
way as beets.

Varieties

Alabaster and Giant
Prague, both mature in
120 days.

<u>Celtuce</u>

This little Known and
seldom grown vegetable is
strictly a home garden
item. It was found in
western China and seeds
were first brought to
American gardens by W.A.
Burpee Company. The name
was chosen because it
combines the uses of
<u>cel</u>ery and let<u>tuce</u>.

This two-purpose vegetable is related to lettuce and grown the same way. But the leaves have four times as much Vitamin C as regular head lettuce. Easily grown, it reaches a height of 12-16 inches in two and a half months.

Seeds are planted in the spring in rows 16 inches apart. Plants are thinned to 8 inches apart in the row. You can plant a few seeds every couple of weeks for a continuous harvest. Young leaves can be used when only a few weeks old. But the real harvest comes when the seed stalks mature.

The stalk is first stripped of its leaves and then peeled of its bitter, outer layer. It has a sweet, juicy, lettuce/celery flavor and is good raw as an appetizer or cooked and served with butter or cream sauce.

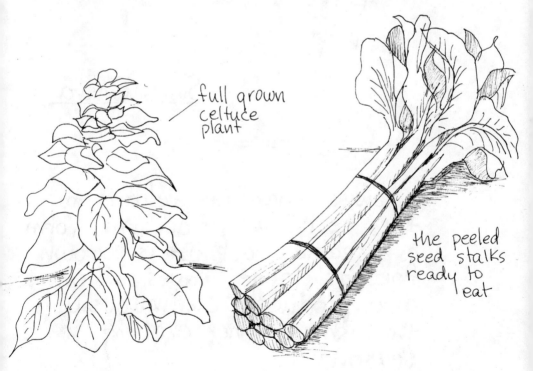

full grown celtuce plant

the peeled seed stalks ready to eat

Swiss Chard

Swiss Chard is related to the beet but it doesn't form a useable root. It is grown for its large leaves which are produced continuously throughout the growing season.

Chard is one of the easiest vegetables to grow withstanding both hot weather and light frost.

It is one of the best tasting greens for summer use and is a good hot weather substitute for spinach since spinach gives up when the heat comes. It is seldom seen at the store because it wilts soon after cutting. This is of no concern to the home gardener who can eat it crisp and fresh. The leaves can be eaten raw in salads or cooked like spinach. And the leafstalks can be eaten raw like celery or cooked and served like asparagus.

Planting can be done as soon as the soil is workable in the spring. It matures in only 60 days. Seeds should be planted ½ inch deep in rows spaced 18 inches apart. The plants are first thinned to 3-4 inches apart. When they begin to crowd, every other plant should be removed. The thinnings can be eaten as greens or transplanted to form additional rows. One planting will produce for the entire season. Any good garden soil will yield a bumper crop. One packet of seeds is sufficient to plant 25 feet of row which should be more than enough for most families.

Varieties

Fordhook Giant, Lucullus, and Rhubarb Chard, which has red leaves and stalks. All mature in 60 days. Rhubarb Chard is attractive enough to plant in a flower garden.

Harvesting

In the home garden chard is harvested by cutting off the outside leaves 1 or 2 inches from the ground. Be careful not to injure new leaves coming from the bud or center of the plant. If only the outer leaves are cut, chard will continue to produce on a "cut and come again" basis for the entire season. Entire plants may even be cut off a couple of inches from the ground and new growth will result. Any surplus may be canned or frozen.

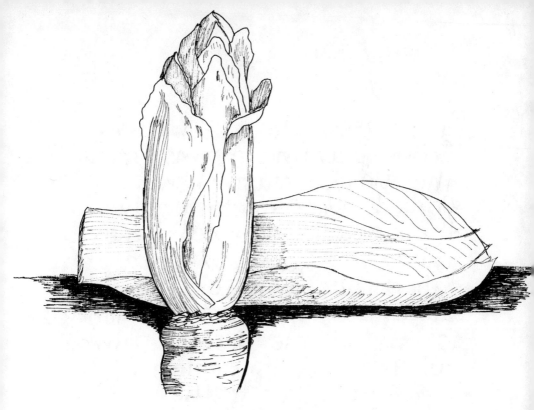

Chicory

   Chicory, also called
French endive, witloof chicory,
and Belgium endive, is
native to Europe and Asia.
It is grown for the roots
which are used for "forcing"
during the Winter. When
seen at the market, which
is rare, it usually sells
for extremely high prices.

It takes 3½ to 4 months from planting to maturity. The plants must then be forced indoors to produce the small blanched heads. The long wait and extra labor account for its high price. But the fact is chicory is one of the easiest plants to grow. It is really a weed, similar to the dandelion, and not at all troubled by insects.

Seeds are planted in Spring or early Summer in rows spaced 15 inches apart, with plants thinned to 6 inches apart within the row. Any good, deeply worked soil will produce fine roots for forcing. Young leaves and thinnings may also be used for salads.

After a few frosts, at the approach of cold weather, the roots are dug up and the tops cut off 2 inches above the stem. Roots are then stored in a cold place until needed.

Forcing

A basement or cellar with a temperature between 50-65 degrees would be ideal. Cut all the roots to a uniform length of 8-9 inches. Stand the roots upright, close together, in boxes of soil, sand, or peat moss. The fertility of the soil is of no consequence as all the energy for forcing is stored in the root. Water the roots

and then cover with 5-6
inches of dry sand or
sawdust. Covering the roots
excludes the light and
keeps the head solid and
compact. In 3-4 weeks
the plants will push up
a head and will be ready
to eat.
Cut the
head off
at the
base.
If roots are
brought in from cold storage
as needed, a continuous
harvest may be enjoyed
all Winter.
　　Chicory roots can
also be roasted in a slow
oven until dry and then
ground and used as a
coffee substitute or adulterant.

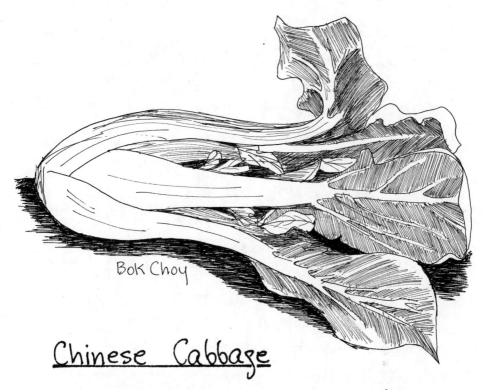

Bok Choy

Chinese Cabbage

Sometimes called celery cabbage, Chinese cabbage resembles romaine lettuce more than ordinary cabbage, both in taste and appearance. It is native to China and has been cultivated there since the 5th century. It is used as a salad green and, especially in Chinese cuisine, as a cooked vegetable.

Chinese cabbage requires a very rich soil, lots of moisture, and a cool growing season. Make the soil as rich as possible with manure or compost. It can be planted in the earliest spring to mature before hot weather but is usually more successful as a fall crop.

Seeds should be planted directly in the garden in rows two feet apart. Seedlings do not transplant well but if care is taken and plants are not too large, less than 6 inches high, it can be done successfully.

Michihli

It is important to prevent any check in growth because the plants will go to seed before forming a head. They must make steady growth and not suffer from a lack of water or soil nutrients.

As a Fall crop seeds are planted around July 1st where the crop is to mature. After plants become well established they are thinned to stand one foot apart in the row. The thinnings can be used as greens. When plants are large enough they will benefit by a mulch to prevent weeds and to keep the soil moist and cool.

Varieties

Pakchoi, or bokchoy as it is also known, is a loose leaf variety resembling Swiss chard in shape. It grows 7-8 inches tall with spoon-shaped leaves. This variety does well as a Spring crop in our garden and is ready to eat in only 45 days. It is listed in the Burpee catalog as Crispy Choy Loose-Leaved Chinese cabbage.

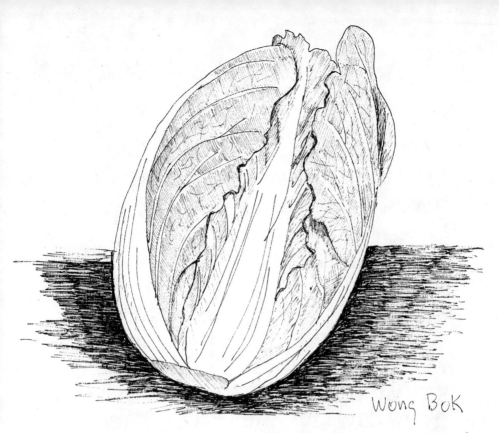

Wong Bok

Burpee Hybrid and Early Hybrid G are Wong-Bok types. They grow to a height of 10-12 inches and are almost as large around. They form a cylindrical head that blanches itself white in the center. Mature 70-75 days.

Michihli grows 18 inches tall and about 4 inches

around. It is an improved strain of the Chihli type and matures in 70 days.

Harvesting

Heads are harvested as needed after they mature. Plants will withstand quite heavy frost and can be left in the garden until late fall. It is customary to remove the outside leaves and discard them to the compost heap. Heads can be kept for a month in a cold cellar with the roots packed in moist soil. They will also keep well in the refrigerator for a couple of weeks. Freeze them for winter use.

<u>Collards</u>

Collards are an important green vegetable in the southern part of the country. Full of vitamins with very few calories, they are grown in place of cabbage which doesn't withstand as much heat nor as much cold. They will grow to perfection in the North too. They are winter hardy in all but the extreme North.

The edible part is the rosette of green leaves at the top of the plant which resembles cabbage just before heading. Seeds can be planted anytime up until mid-summer and the best collards have been sweetened by a touch of frost. They are grown like other cabbage crops. But they will do well in all kinds of soil since they are less fussy.

Plants should be spaced 18-24 inches apart within the row with rows spaced 2½ to 3 feet apart.

For small plants, space them 8 inches apart within the row.

Varieties

Vates, 75 days. They are dwarf-growing, more compact than other varieties. Georgia, 75 days. Grows 2-3 feet tall.

Harvesting

The most common method is to cut off the mature head. Another method is to cut the entire plant when only ¼ grown. This provides the tenderest leaves for salads and cooking.

Corn

Sweet corn is strictly
an American delicacy. Seldom
seen in Europe, the plant
is so common here that
it hardly needs description.
We have all heard tales
of how the American
Indians taught the early
settlers how to plant corn,
placing a fish in each
hill for fertilizer.

In recent years plant breeders have given us some excellent varieties, quick-maturing hybrids with outstanding quality as well as built in disease resistance. Corn is tender to frost and growth is best in hot weather, but with some of the new varieties it can even be raised successfully in such cold climates as Alaska and Newfoundland.

It will grow on a wide range of soil types and is not as fussy as some of the other garden vegetables. But for best results the land should be well-fertilized. By planting early, midseason, and late maturing kinds all at the same time, you can enjoy fresh corn at its best for several weeks from only one planting.

Corn takes a lot of space, but for small gardens you can choose some of the dwarf varieties. And, if space is no problem, you can even grow your own popcorn.

Corn is injured by frost and should be planted when the danger of hard freezing is over. To get corn early in the season home gardeners often take a chance and plant a little earlier than considered safe.

Prepare the soil by adding manure and rock

phosphate and a nitrogen fertilizer such as blood meal, soya meal, or cotton-seed meal. It takes ¼ lb. of seed to plant 100 feet of row. Corn should be planted in blocks of at least three rows side by side rather than in one long row. This is necessary for good pollination for well-filled ears.

   Corn may be planted in hills or in rows. For hill planting, place 5 to 6 seeds one inch deep in a group and thin to the three strongest plants. Space hills 2½ feet apart each way. For rows, plant the seed one inch deep and 4 inches apart, spacing the rows 2 feet apart. Thin the plants to stand 8 to 12 inches apart.

You can plan on harvesting one or two good ears from each plant. Maturity from seed planting usually takes 55 days to 90 days, depending on the weather and the variety. Thrifty gardeners often plant winter squash and pumpkins between the hills or rows of corn. We have even seen farmers in Mexico plant pole beans to climb the corn stalks and

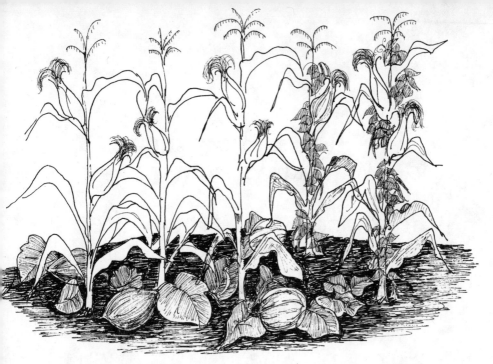

both seemed to do well,
possibly benefitting each
other. (The beans might
supply the extra nitrogen
for the corn and also
shade the roots, keeping
the soil moist.) It used
to be common practice to
pull off the suckers which
form at the sides of the
stalks. However, it has been
proven that these suckers
are necessary to the plants.

So just leave them alone and the plants will be happy.

Popcorn is grown the same way as sweet corn. The only difference is that popcorn is allowed to thoroughly ripen and mature on the plant. Then the ears are brought inside to dry further. After about a month the kernels should be dry and the corn husked. Take the kernels off the cob and store in glass jars in a dry place.

Varieties

There are so many varieties offered by seed men — yellow, white, and the bicolors — that gardeners find it difficult to make a selection. In addition to some of our old favorites, we usually try one or two new varieties each year.

Yellow Corn:

Good home garden varieties include: Polar Vee, 50 days, the earliest maturing corn for very cool regions. Royal Crest, 58 days. Golden Midget, 65 days. Extra-Early-Super-Sweet, 67 days, twice as sweet as other varieties. Should be planted away from other corns as it will lose some sweetness if cross pollinated by other varieties. Golden Beauty, 70 days.

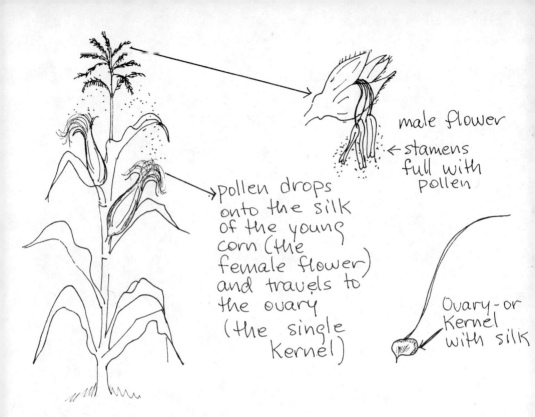

male flower

← stamens full with pollen

pollen drops onto the silk of the young corn (the female flower) and travels to the ovary (the single Kernel)

ovary - or Kernel with silk

Bi-colored:
These have both white and yellow Kernels on each ear. Sugar + Gold, 67 days. Butter + Sugar, 73 days. Honey + Cream, 78 days.

White Corn:
Silver Sweet, 65 days. White midget, 74 days. Burpee's Snowcross, 83 days.

Silver Queen, 92 days.

Popcorn:
    Minhybrid, 83 days.
Tom Thumb, 85 days.
Japanese Hulless, 95 days.

    The gaily colored ornamental corn is grown strictly for decoration.

Harvesting
    Sweet corn should be harvested in the "milk stage". The kernels will be plump and a milky liquid will squirt out if punctured with your thumbnail. At this stage the sugar content is highest. Don't let them get past this stage since the sugar

content decreases and turns to starch, becoming tough. As harvest time approaches the silks will turn brown and will dry slightly. Keep a close watch over your crop especially during hot weather.

Corn loses its sweetness very quickly after harvesting. Pick it just before dinner time and try to have the water boiling before going out. For a taste treat, try roasting the husked ears in the oven at 450° for 15 minutes, turning occasionally.

To freeze corn for out of season enjoyment drop the husked ears into boiling water for 5 minutes

and cool immediately in
ice cold water. Then place
in plastic bags in the
freezer.
    Since we live in a
rural area, racoons are
troublesome at times. They
have an uncanny ability
to know when the corn
is ripe. They do their damage
at night and unfortunately
I don't know of any way
to discourage them except,
perhaps, to move the family
dog out to the corn patch
for a few nights.

Corn Salad

Corn salad is a mildly flavored green used for cooking and as a raw vegetable in salads. More often seen in Europe, it should be given a try here. Sometimes called fetticus or lambs lettuce, it can be recognized by its small spoon-shaped gray-green leaves. It is usually mixed with more pungent greens as the flavor is rather uninteresting when served alone. The tender leaves are often used in place of lettuce in the early Spring from overwintered plants started from seed the previous Fall.

Corn salad should be planted in the early Spring or in late Summer for Fall harvest and overwintering. These plants are hardy and don't like hot weather. Plant the seeds in rows 16 inches apart and thin the plants to 6-8 inches apart within the row.

About a month after planting, leaves can be used for salads. Older plants are good for cooking. Keep the weeds down by cultivating or mulching, and water if needed.

Cucumbers

Cucumbers are members of the Cucurbit family, tender, annual plants grown for their fruit. Melons and squashes are also included in this family. The cucumber is native to Asia and

Africa and has been a cultuated plant there for at least 3,000 years. They grow on vines which take up a lot of room in a small garden but since cucumbers are natural climbers they can be trained to a fence or trellis and will grow up, saving a lot of space.

Both male (staminate) and female (pistillate) flowers are produced on the same plant with staminate outnumbering pistillate sometimes as much as 10 to 1. Only the pistillate flowers will produce fruits. Nature is sometimes overgenerous and plant breeders have succeeded in producing plants with only female blossoms (gynoecious). These hybrids are able to produce enormous yields compared to older varieties. These "all female" hybrids are also amazingly disease resistant — making them very dependable producers.

They are warm season plants and are killed by even a light frost. But they mature so quickly (50-60 days) they can be grown virtually any-where. Seeds will not

germinate in a cold soil
so planting should be
delayed until all danger of
frost is past and the soil
is warm. The soil should
be very rich and able to
hold large amounts of water.
Since cucumbers consist of
95% water, irrigation might
be needed if rainfall is
lacking.

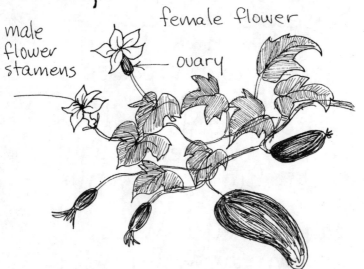

male
flower
stamens

female flower

ovary

If you want an extra-early crop seeds can be started indoors 3-4 weeks before the frost free date. It is important to have the plants placed in individual containers so the roots won't be disturbed when they are set out. Jiffy pots, plant bands, milk containers, or tin cans work well.

Planting can be done in "hills" which are groups of seeds planted together. Don't be confused by this term. Seeds are still planted level and not in raised mounds of soil. Or they can be planted in rows. Each hill should

be about a foot wide dug
to a depth of approximately
one foot, replacing some of
the soil with compost or
manure. Place about a half
dozen seeds in a group,
spacing the seeds a few
inches apart. Plant them
one inch deep with the
pointed ends of the seeds
facing down. Select the
best 2 or 3 well spaced
plants in each hill and
discard the rest. It is best
to cut or pinch off the
unwanted plants instead

cucumber hills

of pulling them up. These
hills should be spaced 4 feet
apart in all directions.
    Planting in "hills" is
still common, but planting
in rows has the advantage
of better plant distribution.
Dig a trench about 6 inches
deep with manure or
compost placed at the
bottom. Seeds are planted
with the points down and
thinned to 1 to 2 feet apart
within the row. Rows are
spaced 4 to 5 feet apart.
If seeds are planted at
two different depths, say
at one and two inches,
an earlier planting is
possible. If the shallow
plants are frosted the
deeper plants, which come up

later, will usually escape the frost. If they both come up, select the planting which shows the most promise.

Cultivation should be frequent and shallow until the vines cover the ground. Avoid injuring or moving the vines as this will reduce yield. When the vines start to "run", spread a mulch since cultivation now will do more harm than good.

Varieties

Two distinct types of cucumbers are grown. "Picklers", which stay small, and "slicers", but they can

be used interchangeably.
We have selected the
Gynoecious Hybrids as the
best of the modern, disease
resistant types. Seed
companies include a
pollinating variety, usually
stained a different color,
in the seed packet.

Pickling varieties:
Mariner, 53 days; Crusader,
51 days; Pioneer, 51 days;
Spartan Dawn, 50 days.

Slicing varieties:
Victory, 62 days; Princess,
63 days; and Gemini, 61 days.

Novelty Cucumbers:
Burpless Hybrid (grows 8-10
inches long), 60 days. This
one is so mild it can be
eaten by people who
experience indigestion with

ordinary cucumbers.

Lemon, 65 days. This variety grows to about the same size and color as a lemon. It has a sweet flavor with a tang of lemon. It can be used for slicing but it also makes excellent sweet pickles. It is grown the same way as other cukes.

Armenian Long and China, 75 days. These kinds grow to amazing lengths— up to 2 feet long and rather slim. Very good quality for the home gardener looking for something to brag about. They should be grown on a fence or trellis to get straight fruit, on the ground

they tend to curve and
twist into odd shapes.

<u>Harvesting</u>

Frequent picking
increases the size of the
yield. They are picked at
various sizes for the
purposes intended. For
slicing, pick them when

they are 6-8 inches long.
Small sizes are good for
pickling. Fruits should not
be left on the vines to
mature as this causes the
vines to concentrate all
its energy on maturing
the seed instead of fruit
production. Be careful
when picking to avoid
injuring the vines.
Don't forget to plant dill
for pickling!

Eggplant

    This heat-loving, tropical vegetable is a perennial but is cultivated as an annual in the North. The plants are particularly attractive and make a handsome addition to the garden. Although the flavor doesn't appeal to everyone, it does serve as a substitute for meat in many countries because of its flavor.

The eggplant is a native of India and belongs to the Nightshade family. Potatoes, tomatoes, and peppers, are also included in this family although eggplant needs longer to mature and demands more heat to ripen its fruit. They can be injured by cool weather and any check in growth results in a poor crop. The plants are bushy, with pretty, purple flowers, sometimes

attaining a height of
2-4 feet and a spread
of almost as much.
     Eggplant takes about
five months from seed
planting until the fruits
ripen. So, in the North,
seeds must be started
inside 8-10 weeks before
being planted outdoors.
Since only a few plants
are needed by most
families, gardeners find
it simplest to buy them at
a reliable nursery, rather
than start them. However,
if you would like to start
a few plants, seeds should
be planted indoors or in
a hotbed or greenhouse.
One packet of seed will
produce more than enough
plants.

Cover the seeds lightly with ¼ inch of fine soil or peat moss. It will take 2-3 weeks for seeds to germinate. During this time they should be kept warm at a temperature between 70-90 degrees. At colder temperatures seeds will not germinate and are likely to rot. It is best to have plants growing in individual containers such as compressed peat pots, which can be set in the garden, pot and all. This avoids any danger of injuring the roots, sometimes called transplant shock.

Plants are set out after all danger of frost is past and the soil is thoroughly warm. Nothing is gained by planting earlier as the plants will only mope along and are likely to be stunted. The best soil is a sandy loam since it warms up quickly. However, clay soils can be used and we find it helpful to mulch the plants with black plastic to warm up our normally cold clay soil.

Plants should be spaced 2½ feet apart within the row, allowing 3 feet between rows. Water thoroughly after the plants are set out.

One or two supplemental feedings with liquid manure will help to increase productivity.

Varieties

Early Beauty Hybrid, 62 days. Burpee Hybrid, 70 days. Mission Bell, 70 days.

For something different you can grow: Applegreen Eggplant, 75 days. It has a green skin which doesn't required peeling. And White Beauty, 80 days, which gives white fruits of mild flavor.

(Days to maturity are calculated from the time plants are set out.)

Harvesting

Eggplants are edible from the time they are ⅓ grown until fully mature. They are best when the skin has a high gloss and remain edible for some time after they are fully grown. But don't wait too long because the seeds will mature and turn bitter. Young fruits are tastiest. Frequent harvesting will encourage the plants to continue producing.

The fruits should be cut from the plants with a knife since the stems are hard and woody. Watch out for the prickly stickers. Be careful not to injure the fruits since they are very perishable when bruised. They can be stored for a few months in a cool place.

Endive

Endive is grown as a salad plant and also used as a cooking green. It is sometimes confused with witloof chicory or French endive, as both belong to the chicory or compositae family. Two distinct types are grown:

the curly-leaf type and the broad leaf kind known as escarolle. It is grown mainly for Fall and Winter use, although it can also be used as an early Summer crop if seeds are planted early in the Spring. For Fall crops seeds are planted in July or August.

The plants make their best growth during cool weather. They are hardy and can withstand light frosts as well as heat. They have requirements similar to lettuce and are less likely to bolt to seed during hot weather.

Seeds should be planted one half inch deep in rows spaced 1½ feet apart. Thin the plants to 10-12 inches apart within the row. Rapid growth results in crisp tender leaves. The soil should be enriched with manure or compost and watered if the soil dries out. One packet of seeds will plant 20 feet of row and will mature in 3 months.

Blanching

Although
not absolutely
necessary, the leaves should
be blanched to reduce their
bitterness and to make
them more tender. Blanching
also improves their appearance,
especially if used for
garnishing, but some loss
in vitamins results.
Blanching takes 2-3 weeks
or somewhat longer in
cool weather. When the
plants are almost fully
grown, or about 12-15 inches
in diameter, all the leaves
are gathered up over the
head into a bunch and
tied near the top. Choose
a day when the leaves are

dry for this task. If rainy weather follows the tying, plants will have to be untied until they are dry again. Then they are retied to continue blanching. After the inside leaves are blanched, the plants will have to be harvested quickly to prevent decay.

Varieties

Green Curled, 90 days. Salad King, 98 days. Full Heart Batavian (escarolle), 90 days.

Harvesting

Unblanched heads can be left in the garden

and used as needed. They can withstand light frost, but they should be protected against severe freezing. Cover the plants with hay, blankets, burlap bags, or anything handy. At the approach of very cold weather, the entire plants can be dug with the soil around the roots and placed in a cool basement or garage. So treated, the plants can be kept for several months. In mild climates, plants can be left in the garden all winter.

Herbs

The herb gardener's reward comes in the form of sweet aromas and savory meals. The pungent leaves and seeds can be used fresh, dried, or frozen. We are listing thirteen herbs that we have grown for culinary purposes, although there are many more with other uses.

Herbs require little care and are not the least bit tempermental about the soil. It is even said that poor soil results in aromatically stronger plants. Most of the annual kinds of herbs are raised from seed and some of the perennials can be purchased as small plants from most seed companies.

In general, herbs grown for their leaves are used fresh. For winter use they must be dried or frozen. Gather the leaves when the plants are flowering and hang them in a cool, dry place with good air circulation. Keep them out of the sun as this will quickly fade their fresh, green color. When dry, the leaves should be stored in lightly covered glass jars.

Herbs grown for their seeds should be harvested when ripe but before the seeds start to fall from the stems. Place the seed stalks on some clean newspaper or in paper bags until thoroughly dry. Then seperate the seeds from the chaff and store.

Basil

Basil is a strongly aromatic annual with a clovelike flavor and a sweet, spicy odor. It is cherished by the Italians since it combines so well with tomatoes. The leaves are also used in salads, meat, and fish dishes. Basil vinegar is made by steeping the fresh leaves in a bottle of vinegar for about 2-3 weeks.

Only a few plants are needed by most families. Seeds are planted after the ground is warm, spacing plants 4 inches apart. Harvest the leaves as the plants are just coming into bloom.

Cut the stems but leave
an inch or two on the
plants so that growth may
continue.

Chervil

Chervil, or
French parsley, is
often called the
gourmet's parsley. It is a
delicately flavored herb
suggesting a hint of anise.
A tender annual, it grows
about 1 foot tall with fernlike
leaves. Since we planted this
herb some years ago it has
appeared all over the garden
every year from self-sown
seeds. It grows best in a
moist well-drained soil either
in sun or shade.
Plant the seeds any

time until midsummer and harvest the leaves as needed. Easily dried, the leaves retain their flavor best when frozen. To freeze, place the fresh leaves in a closed glass jar in the freezer. What could be simpler?

Coriander

Coriander is an annual growing about 2 ft. tall. The leaves look a little like Italian parsley and can be used in the same way. Coriander has been cultivated since ancient times. It was used by the Greeks and Romans both as a medicinal

and as a meat preservative.
It was claimed also to be
a powerful aphrodisiac and
was used to summon the
devil.

The dried seeds are
used in cookies, cakes, candies,
curry powder, sausage, and
in mixed pickling spices.
Plant the seeds in the early
Spring and thin the plants
to 8-10 inches apart. Harvest
the seeds promptly when
mature, or they may fall
and be lost.

Dill

Dill is a hardy
annual familiar
to us all
because it is
used to flavor dill pickles.

But its use is not limited to pickles. The leaves can be put to use in soup, egg dishes, with fish, and in salads. They can also be made into a delicious vinegar much the same way as basil.

Plant the seeds in the spring and thin the plants to 1 foot apart each way. Dill grows about 3 feet tall and should be grown in full sun. Harvest the fresh leaves as needed. Since the leaves lose almost all their flavor when dried, we freeze a supply for winter because frozen dill retains all the flavor of the fresh product. Harvest the seeds as soon as they are ripe. If a few seeds fall to the ground, the plant will self-sow and save you the trouble of having to plant it next year.

Lovage

This seldom seen herb used to be a favorite in colonial gardens. It is a very hardy perennial growing 3-5 feet tall. The leaves resemble celery both in appearance and taste. Leaves are fine in soup, salad, sauces, brewed into tea, or anywhere a celery flavor is desired. The English make a confection out of the seeds by coating them with sugar. Lovage will do well in full sun or partial shade.

It is a rather coarse-looking plant whose leaves turn yellow in Fall. Plant the seeds in the Spring and space the plants 18 inches apart. Only one or two plants are needed since they will form a huge clump in a year or two. In our garden this plant has been one of the most dependable herbs along with chives.

Sweet Marjoram

Sweet marjoram is a perennial but is grown as an annual in the North since it is not hardy enough to live through the Winter. The leaves are used fresh or dry in soup, stuffings, fish, lamb, and they are sometimes brewed into tea. The plants grow about 1 foot tall and should be spaced about 6 inches apart. Seeds are sometimes slow to germinate, so we start a few plants indoors and set them out when the ground is warm. Small plants may be brought indoors and grown in a sunny window over the Winter.

Mints

The mint family includes the familiar peppermint, spearmint, orangemint, apple mint, lemon balm, catnip, pennyroyal, and a few others. All mints are easy to grow. In fact, you must be careful because they spread too quickly and can crowd out other plants.

They do best in a rich, moist soil in sun or shade. Space the plants 1 foot apart. Mints can be grown from seed or from root cuttings. Clumps should be divided every few years to keep them growing vigorously. In many parts of the country mints have escaped cultivation and are found growing wild. They are easy to recognize since they have square stems and a characteristic odor. If you find some wild mint that you particularly like

bring back a few roots for
the garden.

Sage

Sage is a
hardy perennial
but has never
survived our 40°
below winters. Since we need
only two or three plants we
usually start them inside
in the Spring and repot them
in the Fall to overwinter in
a sunny window. The plant
grows 3 feet tall but we cut
them back to keep them in
bounds. They require little care,
although they should be grown
in full sun, spaced 1 foot apart.
Several crops can be
harvested for drying.

Cut the leaves before the plants bloom, and dry indoors on trays or hang up the leaves until dry.

Parsley

Parsley is the most popular of all the herbs and the flavor is so familiar it hardly needs description. It is easy to grow but the seeds are slow to germinate. Soak the small seeds in water for a couple of hours before planting them. Seeds can be planted outside as soon as the soil is workable or they can be started indoors.

There are several varieties of parsley: the curly leaf, which is the most popular especially for garnishing; the plain leaf, sometimes called Italian parsley; and the Hamburg or turnip rooted parsley, which is grown for its root. We use a lot of parsley fresh, having found the dried leaves lacking in flavor. The best way to have "fresh" parsley for Winter is to freeze it.

Summer Savory

Summer Savory is a quickly growing annual

which often self-sows. It has a pleasant flavor that combines well with all bean dishes, fish, soup, stuffing, sauces, and rice. The plant grows to 1-1½ feet tall and has inconspicuous pale, pink flowers.

In our climate and location we plant seeds directly in the garden in full sun during the first week of June. Seeds germinate in about 2 weeks and plants should be spaced 6 inches apart. Cut the whole plant when it starts to flower and dry indoors. When thoroughly dry, pull off the leaves and store in tightly covered glass jars.

Tarragon

The French tarragon, dracunculus sativus, is an herb for connoiseurs. It is propogated only by root divisions. There is a Russian variety, artemisia redowski, which can be grown from seed, but it is vastly inferior and has a bitter flavor. Make sure of getting the true French tarragon.

Obtain two or three plants from a seedsman or greenhouse. Plant them in full sun, in well-drained soil. Space the plants 1 foot apart. They grow to a height of 2-3 feet. Harvest the young leaves as needed and dry a supply for winter. The leaves are used to flavor chicken, fish, salads, vinegars, and soups.

Thyme

There are many varieties of thyme, including the narrow-leafed French thyme. But the best variety for culinary use is the broad-leafed English thyme. This hardy perennial grows well from seed.

Plant in full sun, spacing the plants 8 inches apart. Since it is low-growing it can also be grown in a rock garden or can be used as an edging plant. Thyme is strongly flavored and should be used sparingly.

Just a pinch improves the flavor of stuffings, soups, pork, and it can be brewed into tea. Cut the stems for drying just before the plants bloom and store in covered jars.

Watercress

Watercress is a hardy perennial often found growing along the banks of streams and other wet spots, but not in stagnant areas. It can be grown in containers that are kept very moist.

Watercress may be grown from seed, but the simplest way is to buy a bunch at the market and root it in a glass of water. Then transplant it outside.

Horseradish

If you don't mind the tears you can grate your own horseradish. The roots, which look a little like parsnips, add a liveliness to many seafood, vegetable, and meat dishes. It is a hardy perennial and does well in the cooler parts of the country. Although native to Eastern Europe, it is often found growing wild here around old farmhouses, surviving without any care. Left unattended, however, roots will grow woody and it is best to plant new ones every year or two.

The plants grow 2-3 feet tall, bearing small, white flowers. Although seed is produced, it doesn't germinate well and propogation is always done from root cuttings or by dividing the old crowns. Root cuttings are taken from the side roots. They will vary in size from 2-6 inches long and from ¼ to ½ inch in diameter.

These are sold by most seed companies and a half dozen roots should prove ample for most families.

A deeply worked soil is needed to get straight roots. Hard, compacted soil results in crooked, branched roots. Unless the soil is very rich, well-rotted manure should be deeply dug into the area. Plant the cuttings deep enough so that the top is just below the soil surface. The roots should be planted 10-12 inches apart in rows spaced 2½-3 feet apart. Then pack the soil tightly around the cuttings. Planting can be done any time but is most commonly done in the Spring to give a full growing season.

Varieties

Maliner Kren or Bohemian.

Harvesting

Since the roots are very hardy they can be left in the ground all Winter. However, if a supply is wanted it is best to store a few roots before the ground freezes so they will be available when needed. The roots are ready to harvest in September or October from a Spring planting. Leave a few roots or pieces of the root in the ground to furnish a supply of young plants for the following season. Very young leaves may also be eaten early in the spring if you enjoy their peppery flavor. Later on in the season the leaves turn tough and fiery hot.

Horseradish Sauce: The days when the horseradish grinder was a standard kitchen tool are long since gone. But an electric blender does an even better job. Wash and peel the roots and cut them up into chunks. Put them in the blender with some vinegar and salt to taste.

If you find the flavor
is too strong, some raw
beet or turnip can be
added. The sauce will keep
for a long time in the
refrigerator.

Scotch Kale

Kale

Kale or borecole, as it is sometimes called, is a member of the cabbage family, but does not form a head. It most nearly resembles the wild form of cabbage. Kale is perhaps the most decorative member of that family, often used in the flower garden.

It will produce good crops
anywhere in the country
and thrives in cold weather.
In fact, frost actually
improves the flavor.

As a source of vitamins,
Kale has few equals. Its
high content of vitamins
A and C, plus considerable
quantities of thiamine, iron,
and calcium, make it
especially valuable in the
diet. It provides fresh greens
well into the Fall and
early Winter when they
are scarce and most
appreciated.

Kale does not thrive
in hot weather and is
seldom grown as a Summer
crop. It is so extremely
hardy it does well in Alaska

and often survives our cold New England winters. It is usually planted in mid-Summer to replace some earlier vegetable which has finished bearing. Kale thrives under the same conditions as other members of the cabbage family — rich soil, plenty of lime, and lots of water.

Seeds for the Fall and Winter crops are planted in July or August. Where summers are not too hot, Spring planting should be done as early as the soil can be prepared. Seeds are planted in rows spaced 18 inches apart and the plants thinned to 12 inches apart. The plants removed in thinning are useful as greens since they are more tender than older leaves. One packet of seeds will be enough to plant 50 feet of row, probably more than enough to supply the whole neighborhood since kale is such a prolific yielder.

Varieties

Two types of Kale are grown, the Scotch and the Siberian kinds. The Scotch has grey-green leaves which are very curled and the Siberian has leaves which are deep blue-green and not quite as curly. There are also dwarf and tall-growing varieties of each type but the dwarf forms are more popular with home gardeners.

Siberian Kale

Good varieties include:
Dwarf Green Curled, 55 days.
Dwarf Siberian, 65 days.
Tall Green Curled Scotch,
55 days. And Vates, 55 days.

Harvesting

There are two ways of harvesting Kale — mature leaves can be cut as needed, leaving the young inner leaves to mature, or by cutting the entire plant. By picking only the outside leaves, the plants will continue producing on a "cut and come again" basis much the same as chard. For salad greens, the young, inner leaves are preferred since they are much more tender than the outside leaves. Since Kale is so hardy and improved by frost, the plants can be left in the garden and leaves may be harvested as needed by simply brushing the snow off the plants and cutting as desired.

Kohlrabi

Kohlrabi is one of the strangest looking of the vegetables. It belongs to the cabbage family but is not a cabbage, nor is it a turnip. But in many ways it resembles both of them. The name literally means cabbage-turnip. The stem enlarges just above ground into a turnip-shaped globular swelling and is topped by large cabbage-like leaves. Kohlrabi is very popular in Europe and is greatly relished by the Chinese, but it is seldom seen here. The taste can best be described as a sweetly flavored turnip, more tender and superior to it in flavor.

It is a hardy, cool season plant and does best as a Spring and fall crop. Midsummer maturing bulbs are apt to be tough and stringy. It matures quickly, 50-60 days, and can be grown anywhere.

Rapid growth is necessary to produce high quality. A rich soil is needed and this plant really benefits from the addition of large amounts of organic matter.

Seed is planted ½ inch deep in rows spaced 18 inches apart. The seedlings are thinned to stand 6 inches apart within the row. Plant again in late Summer for Fall and Winter use.

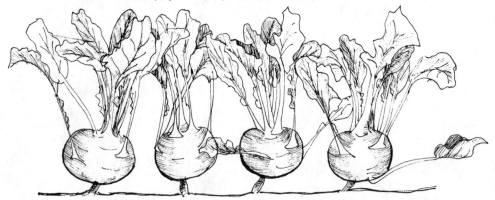

Varieties

The most popular varieties, and usually the only ones listed by seed companies, are Early White Vienna, and Early Purple Vienna, which is similar except for the purple skin — but the flesh of both are white and taste the same.

Harvesting

Kohlrabi should be harvested when young and tender. Not larger than 2-3 inches in diameter. As it grows larger it becomes tough and woody, hardly worth eating at all.

Kohlrabi will keep for several months in a cool place with high humidity.

<u>Leeks</u>

Leeks are a mild-tasting member of the onion family. However, their culture is different from that of the onions. No bulb is formed as in the onion nor a bunch of cloves as in the garlic and shallot. The leek is grown for its blanched stem and also for the leaves, which are good for flavoring many dishes! They are native to the Mediterranean region and have been cultivated for thousands of years, especially by the Greeks and Romans.

Leeks have a thick stem up to two inches in diameter and about 6 inches in length. The blanched stems have a sweet, delicate flavor. They are nice thinly sliced in salads, stews, and soups, especially Vichyssoise (leek and potato soup). They grow slowly, taking 3-4 months to reach maturity. But they can be harvested and enjoyed much earlier as a substitute for scallions.

Although they can be planted directly from seed in the garden, we usually start a flat inside about 2 months before setting out. Seeds are planted ¼ inch deep in flats containing equal parts of loam, sand, compost, or peat moss. Plants should be thinned to 2 inches apart each way. When they are 4-5 inches tall, the plants should be set out in the garden.

For outside planting dig a trench 6-8 inches deep and 4-6 inches wide. Work in an inch or two of compost or well rotted manure into the bottom of the trench and set the plants 6 inches apart. Or, if you prefer, seeds can be planted in the bottom of the trench and thinned to 6 inches apart. Space the rows 18 inches apart. As the plants reach maturity soil should be added gradually to the trench to whiten the stems.

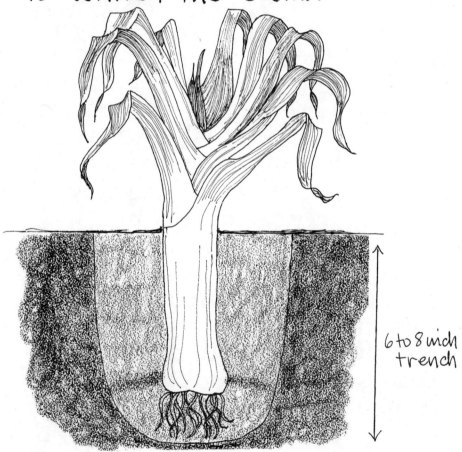

6 to 8 inch trench

Be careful not to bank up the soil too soon since the plants decay easily, especially when young. Try not to get the soil into the leaves which can cause problems cleaning them.

Varieties

All the varieties mature in about 100 days from seed. They are all quite similar in taste, so take your pick: American Flag, Swiss Special, Giant Musselburg, and Unique — which has extra long stems often 8 inches or more.

Harvesting

Leeks are harvested by cutting the roots off at the base. They can be left in the garden all Winter in a warm climate. But here in the North, the crop should be dug before the ground freezes and stored in a cold basement or garage. Contrary to popular belief, they may also be frozen as can all onions.

<u>Vichyssoise</u>: The flavor of the leeks and potatoes combine nicely in this delicious French soup. It may be served hot or cold, but usually cold.

Sauté 2 cups of chopped leeks, including a few green, tender leaves, in butter until transparent but not brown. Add 3 cups of water or chicken stock, 2 cups of diced potatoes, and one stalk of celery, thinly sliced. Cover and simmer until the vegetables are tender. Now, put the soup through a food mill or sieve. Add salt and pepper to taste. Add one cup of heavy cream or evaporated milk and chill. Garnish with chopped dill, parsley, or chives.

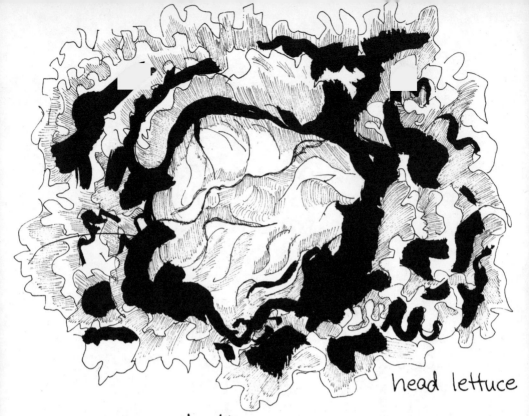

head lettuce

Lettuce

Lettuce is the most popular of all the garden vegetables and grown in nearly every home garden. Native to Europe, it has been cultivated for almost 3,000 years. Various types have been developed from the wild lettuce which grows as a weed throughout

North America. Four main types are grown, the loose-leaf, the familiar head lettuce, the Romaine (sometimes called Cos lettuce), and the butterheads.

The loose-leaf type doesn't form a head — forming instead a thick cluster or rosette of leaves. It is the easiest kind to grow and not as exacting about the weather as the head lettuce. It withstands the heat well and also contains the greatest amount of vitamins.

Head lettuce forms a solid head much like the cabbage. It is the kind most often found at the market. Head lettuce is more difficult to raise as a

Summer crop since it thrives best in cool weather, like all lettuces, but has a tendency to form seed stalks instead of forming a head when the weather turns hot. We have had good results with head lettuce by planting it in a semi-shady part of the garden, sometimes between

loose-leaf

the pea rows or near
the asparagus to provide
the needed relief from
the heat.

The butterhead type
is the best tasting of all
the lettuces and is perfect
for the home garden.
None can match them in
quality. They produce well-
formed heads with creamy,
yellow hearts that look
as good as they taste.

Romaine lettuce forms
tall heads of good quality
and are fairly heat
resistant. They are usually
planted to mature in the
Fall over much of the
country, except where summers
are cool, when they can be
raised all season long.

Butterhead type

One packet of seed
of each type will provide
more than enough. Lettuce
seeds are long-lived and
will remain viable for up
to 5 years. All lettuces
have the same requirements
-- cool, rich soil and lots
of water. They all benefit
from a mulch which helps
to keep the soil cool and
moist. They can be grown
on all kinds of soils from
heavy clays to sandy loams,

doing best when the soil is made as rich as possible with manure or compost. The soil should be well-drained yet able to hold large amounts of water since lettuce has a small root system and can't search too far.

For the earliest crop, seeds can be started indoors 5-6 weeks ahead of outdoor planting time. Since lettuce has a small root system it transplants easily. Plants, as well as seeds, can go in as soon as the soil is workable. Light frost won't harm them. You should plant a few different types which will provide not only variety for the salad bowl but

also a succession of harvests.
Also plant a few seeds
every couple of weeks to
insure a continuous supply.
        Plant the seeds
thinly in rows spaced 14-18
inches apart. Beginning

Cos or Romaine

gardeners often plant lettuce too thickly so thinning should not be delayed. Thin them first to 2 inches apart and when the plants are bite-sized, remove every other one. This way you will be provided with salad material in less than a month from seed planting. Keep eating the thinnings until plants are ultimately spaced 10-12 inches apart. For the best growth plants should not be allowed to touch.

If a mulch is used, cultivation is unnecessary. Otherwise, frequent, shallow cultivation is important because the plants can't compete with weeds. Most of the roots are near

the surface so be careful
not to hoe too deeply.

Varieties

Since lettuce is so
popular, plant breeders have
been hard at work and have
given us well over 100
varieties to choose from.
Most of them, however, have
commercial importance so
we have selected only
those which are highest in
quality and best for home
use.

Loose-leaf: All mature in
40-65 days. Salad Bowl, Black
Seeded Simpson, Oak Leaf,
Green Ice (which is new
for 1973), and Grand Rapids.
Ruby, although not of the

highest quality, does have attractive, red-bronze leaves which add eye appeal to any salad.

<u>Butterhead</u>: All mature in 70-80 days. Our favorite variety, by far, is Buttercrunch. It is similar to the old Bibb lettuce, but is larger and more heat resistant. Big Boston and Dark Green Boston are also hard to beat. Summer Bibb is better suited than regular Bibb for Summer harvesting. Fordhook Lettuce has thick, crunchy leaves and grows more upright than other butterhead types.

<u>Head Lettuce</u>: Great Lakes does well in hot weather, forming extra-large heads. Pennlake, Fulton, Iceburg,

and Ithaca are also fine.
<u>Romaine Lettuce</u>: Parris
Island Cos, 80 days, is the
best variety and grows
about 10 inches tall.

Harvesting

Loose-leaf lettuce can
be harvested any time after
the plants are large enough
to eat. Usually only the outer
leaves are harvested, leaving
the inner leaves to continue
growing. Thinning the plants,
by removing the largest ones
and leaving the smaller ones
to develop, results in a longer
harvest period. Head lettuce
is usually allowed to grow
to full size before harvesting,
although we sometimes snatch
a few leaves from each

plant and this doesn't seem to bother them.

Try to pick lettuce during the cooler parts of the day as the leaves are much crisper then. Wash the leaves and dry them well. Although lettuce is not usually stored for any length of time it can be kept in the refrigerator for a couple of weeks if placed in closed containers or plastic bags.

As often happens, gardeners plant too much

lettuce. You might be surprised to find that lettuce is an excellent cooked green, prepared much like spinach. Since it shrinks when cooked, you can use plenty of it this way.

Marijuana

We include this herb in the event that legislators take an enlightened attitude and once again permit its cultivation. Even George Washington made reference in his writings to the desire to return home for the hemp harvest. Hemp is also known as marijuana, bhang, gage, weed, boo, among others. It is a half-hardy annual belonging to the mulberry family and a native of Asia where it has been cultivated in China for almost 5,000 years. But since its planting here for fiber, it has escaped cultivation and is frequently found growing wild in waste places, vacant lots, and pastures. It was once cultivated in gardens as an ornamental.

In most places there are laws making it a crime to have it growing on ones property. The justification for making it illegal is that a resinous substance is produced on female plants and has certain pleasant, soporific qualities. Male plants produce smaller quantities of the resin. The narcotics bureau has always tried to associate it with hard drugs to create popular sentiment for keeping it illegal, inspite of the fact that hemp is not a narcotic.

Hemp can be easily identified by compound leaves which consist of from 5-7 leaflets. Very small, green flowers are found in the axillary racemes of female plants. The plants are dioecious — male and female occur in separate plants — which is not too common in the plant world. All parts of the plant are useful. The flowers are used for treating cuts and wounds, the seeds are used for their oil and as a stimulating tonic, and the juice from the leaves is said to counteract scorpion and snake bites. Plants can be very useful to organic gardeners since they are powerful insect repellants also.

Despite the fact that it is a weed with amazing vigor, it will only grow "like a weed" when conditions are to its liking. When soil conditions are favorable, marijuana plants can sometimes reach an incredable height of 15 ft. in a single season. But to make a growth of this sort it must have well-prepared, humusy soil, not too acid, with ample plant food. Marijuana is a gross feeder, the quality of the crop, as well as the quantity, is directly related to the amount of nutrients available.

The best soils seem to be loams and sandy loams with perfect drainage. Clay soils are usually too dense to permit adequate root development and are usually not too well drained. If one has no alternative and is forced to use poor soil, he must work in lots of organic matter. Other weeds don't have a chance to compete since hemp grows taller and will quickly overshadow them. Seeds may be started indoors in individual containers a month early, or seeds can be planted directly outdoors. The longer the plants grow the stronger they will be. Plant the seeds ½ inch deep and thin them when 6 inches tall to stand 3-4 ft. apart in all directions. When plants are 1ft. tall, pinch off the top inch of the plant (called the growing point) to produce bushy plants with lots of leaves. Plants should be harvested in the Fall before frost blackens the leaves. The most common way to harvest them is to cut them off at ground level. The next step is to dry the leaves. This is best accomplished by hanging the plants upside down in a dry, airy place. In about a week or less, depending on temperature and humidity, the leaves should be dry. Strip them off the stalks and branches and store the leaves in a dry place to prevent them from molding.

female

male

Melons

Melons belong to the Cucurbit family which includes the squashes, pumpkins, and, of course, the cucumbers. Both the muskmelon, or cantaloupes and the watermelon are tender annual plants which thrive only during hot, dry weather. They will not withstand any frost.

Cool growing weather results
in flat tasting, insipid
fruit. The culture of all
melons is similar.

Melons require more
space in the garden than
most other vegetables and
are not considered easy
to grow in most regions
of North America. It is,
therefore, not practical to
grow them where summers
are short and usually cool.
They develop their highest
flavor in the South and
Southwest and most
commercial production is
limited to those areas. But
a juicy, sweet, vine-ripened,
home-grown melon is
something hard to forget.
The melons sold at the
store are usually picked

green, before they are ripe, and the resulting flavor can never compare to the sweetness of the natural sugar found in dead-ripe, home-grown melons.

Melons can be grown in most types of soils, but where earliness is a prime factor as in the North, a sandy light soil is considered best. Also, choose the quickest maturing varieties. Melons should be grown in the sunniest spot in the garden. Since they are such heavy feeders they must have large amounts of well-rotted manure or compost mixed with the soil. You should mix a shovelful or two of manure into each hill. In the North the usual practice is to start the plants 3-5 weeks early inside. Large peat pots, plant bands, or milk containers, should be used as the plants do not transplant well if the roots are disturbed.

Several seeds are planted in each container, thinning them to the strongest one or two plants after they are established. It is important to transplant while the plants are small, about a month old, or before four leaves have developed. Otherwise the plants will be stunted in their growth or pot bound (outgrowing the container). Wait until the weather turns warm and settled before planting outside.

Melons can be planted in hills or in rows. Hills should be spaced 5-6 feet apart each way for the smaller growing varieties and somewhat further apart for the larger growing kinds. Two plants are set in each hill. Or seeds may be planted directly in the garden in areas where summers are long.

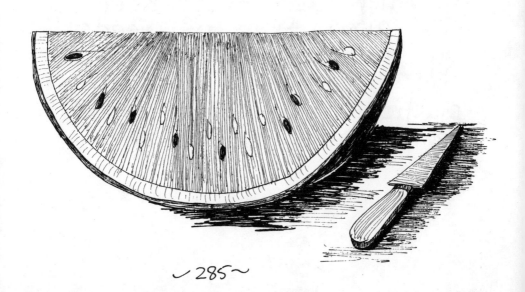

Plant 5-10 seeds with the pointed ends down ½ inch deep. Thin to the two best plants in each hill.

Melons need large amounts of water when the vines are developing, but water should not be given when the fruits are ripening. Usually some sort of protection is placed over the seedlings. Hot caps or plastic tents or portable, home-made cold frames are sometimes used to help warm the soil, protecting the seedlings from cold weather and frost. Keep the area free of weeds by cultivating. Or mulch the area with black plastic to raise the soil temperature for earlier ripening and larger yields.

Varieties

The hybrid varieties of cantaloupe are a good home garden choice. A fine one for the North and Canada is Mainerock Hybrid, ripening in only 75 days. Burpee Hybrid, 82 days, is noted for its fine flavor and dependability. Harper Hybrid, 85 days, is another popular one. Other good varieties are Saticoy Hybrid, 85 days, and Samson Hybrid, 85 days.

Midget or ice-box size watermelons are an ideal choice for home gardeners. Their small size makes them convenient and they are of high quality, maturing early. New Hampshire Midget grows only about 6 inches across, about the same size as a cantaloupe. It matures in only 70 days. A very similar one is Golden Midget, 70 days. The rind of this melon turns yellow when ripe, eliminating much guesswork for the gardener. Sugar Baby grows to about 8 inches across and matures in only 75 days. There is even one which is completely seedless. It is called Triple Sweet Seedless Hybrid, 80 days. But it must be grown with another watermelon since it has to be cross-pollinated.

Harvesting

All melons should be left on the vine until they are fully mature. A fruit is ripe when the stem of the melon will slip away from the vine with only slight pressure from the thumb. This is called the full-slip stage. It it doesn't come off easily, it should be left to ripen further. Some people can select a ripe melon by the aroma, but this comes only after a lot of experience. Melons increase in flavor, but not in sweetness, after harvesting. Remember, fruits picked too soon will never become sweeter.

Mustard

One of the joys of gardening is to grow the unusual, little known vegetables. Mustard is one of them, a hardy annual grown for its leaves, which can be used for cooking or for salads. It seems to be more popular in the south, but for some peculiar reason it is seldom grown

in the North. It grows
extremely quickly and is
ready to eat with the
earliest radishes.

The broad, tender
leaves have a delicious
tang, not too sharp, but
just right to liven up a
salad. Another one of
mustard's virtues is its
extremely high vitamin
content, almost as much
as Kales'.

For the earliest
crop, seeds may be planted
right in the coldframe.
Later plantings can be made
as soon as the soil is
workable, followed by small,
successive plantings until
the weather turns hot.
Then plant again in the
Fall. One packet of seeds

will provide enough for
several plantings.
     The seeds are
planted ½ inch deep within
rows spaced 12 inches
apart. Thin the plants
until they stand 6 inches
apart. These thinnings are
extremely tender and
perfect for salads.

Varieties

     Giant Southern Curled
has tall, broad, curled, and
frilled leaves. Tendergreen
is the fastest growing and
also the most heat and
drought resistant variety.
Burpee's Fordhook Fancy is
mildly flavored and slow
to form seed stalks. All
mature in 30-40 days.

Harvesting

Leaves are cut from the plants as needed. By harvesting frequently, plants are discouraged from flowering and a longer harvest period results. So cut back the plants often. Small leaves, less than 4 inches long, are perfect for salads. Larger ones are better for cooking.

The Onion Family

Onions have been cultivated since ancient times. They belong to the Allium family which includes the common onion, leeks, garlic, chives, shallots, and a few minor species including the ornamental onions. All of them have the typical onion aroma and flavor.

There are also a few wild
onions native to North
America which we search
for every Spring.
      In the home garden
onions are usually grown
from sets or from
young plants. Sets are
small immature onions
grown from thickly
planted seeds the previous
season. These will vary
in size from ½ inch to
1 inch in diameter with
the smaller size considered
best since large ones
tend to produce seed
stalks before forming
bulbs. Sets will produce
young green onions
(scallions) in about a month,
or they may be left to

mature and produce large onions in 3 months.

Young onion plants which have been grown during the Winter in the South (mostly Texas) are shipped north during the Spring, enabling northern gardeners to raise the large Sweet Spanish and Bermuda type onions which would not normally mature in time from seed. These are available at the right planting time from most seed companies, costing about $1.00 a bunch (usually 100 plants).

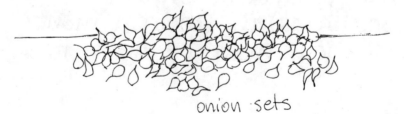

onion sets

Although onions can be raised from seed, they are considered somewhat of a hassle, especially when only a small quantity is needed. (But seed offers a wider choice of varieties, however.) The use of sets or plants, instead of seeds, usually results in an earlier, larger yield, eliminating the labor involved in thinning.

All onions are very hardy and should be planted as early as the soil can be prepared. Light freezes do not harm

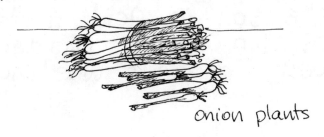

onion plants

them. They may be grown
on almost all types of
soil, but they must have
good drainage. Onions have
a small root system and
need an abundant supply
of easily available
nutrients in the topsoil.
Humus material in the
soil not only feeds the
plants but also keeps
the moisture in, which is
vital since onions need
a steady growth and
must not be checked
at any time.

The soil should be
thoroughly prepared and
lime should be added if
the soil is acid. A pH
of 6.0-6.5 is considered
best. Frequent weeding

is most important since the plants cannot compete with weeds. All onions will benefit from a mulch, especially if it is compost or well-rotted manure.

Sets and plants should be spaced 3-4 inches apart in rows spaced 12-15 inches apart. Seeds are planted thickly and are thinned to the same distance after they have grown a couple of inches tall. Thinnings are used as scallions. One pound of onion sets will plant 50 feet of row. The sets are planted about one inch deep and lightly covered so that the tops are just level with the soil surface. Plants, on the other hand, are placed as shallowly as possible so that they just manage to stand up straight. If seeds are used, cover them with less than ½ inch of fine soil.

Varieties

Onions come in three distinct colors: red, white, and yellow. Yellow onions are the most popular, accounting for over 3/4 of the commercial crop. The most popular varieties include: Sweet Spanish and Sweet Spanish Hybrid, 110 days; Yellow Globe Hybrid, 100 days; Ebenezer, 105 days, which is grown most often for sets. Southport Red Globe and Red Burgundy, 100 days, are popular red onions.

Harvesting

As the onion matures

it is helpful to loosen and draw the soil away from each bulb. This allows them room to develop to a much larger size than normally. When they have reached full maturity the tops will begin to wither and fall over. Any tops that remain standing can be bent down, which will hasten ripening. Pull the onions up and put them in a dry place for about a week or until the tops are thoroughly dry. Then cut the tops off, leaving an inch or two of stem attached. If cut too close, an opening will be left

through which decay may enter.

Onions need cool, dry storage with good air circulation around the bulbs. Mesh sacks and open crates or boxes are often used. Or the tops may be braided together and hung up which also makes for decorative storage. You can hang them in your kitchen this way. Immature and thick-necked onions should be used first, as these will not keep well.

Garlic and Shallots

These differ from the onion in that they produce bulbs containing 6-10 or

more cloves to each bulb.
Seeds are not planted.
Instead, each bulb is
separated into cloves which
are planted and cared
for exactly like onion
sets. Garlic is much more
pungent than onion and
is used mainly as a
flavoring. Shallots are much
more delicately flavored
than onions, but are
somewhat more tedious to

prepare. They are also stored in the same way as onions.

<u>Chives</u>

Chives are a very common, hardy, perennial herb belonging to the onion family. The plants form thick tufts of grass-like foliage with attractive, purple flowers. They produce tiny bulbs which grow in tight clusters. Plant the clumps a foot apart. Only the leaves are used to give a delicate onion flavor which combines well with many foods. The leaves are cut off with a scissors or a knife. Frequent cutting stimulates tender, new growth to appear.

Since seed is seldom used, plants are propagated by dividing established clumps which should be done every 3-4 years to keep them vigorous. They may also be grown year round in a sunny window.

Parsnips

Although not everyone's favorite, parsnips are easily grown and generally free of insects and disease. They have a distinctive flavor, not easily forgotten. They require a long growing season, about 4 months, and can be grown anywhere in the country. The best flavor is developed after the plants have gone through a couple of frosts, which changes the starch into sugars.

A rich soil, deeply worked, is best for developing long, straight roots. Since they are a long-season crop and not injured by frost, the seeds should be planted very thickly, as early as possible.

One packet of seeds will provide enough to supply even the most ardent parsnip lover. Plant the seeds in beds much the same as with beets and carrots, or plant in rows. Cover the seeds with 1/4 inch of fine soil or sand. Seeds are slow to germinate, often taking 3 weeks to come up. Therefore, it is a good idea to plant a few radish seeds along with the parsnips to mark the area for cultivation. Parsnip seeds are short-lived so only fresh seeds should be planted. Don't keep them from year to year.

Thin the plants to stand 4-6 inches apart. It is important to keep the weeds down by frequent hoeing when the plants are small and delicate. As soon as the plants are large enough, spread a mulch.

Varieties

All mature in 100-120 days. Very few varieties have been developed. Harris Model, All America, and Hollow Crown are fine.

Harvesting

Parsnips are harvested in the Fall after a few frosts which improve their quality. Any excess can be left in the ground all Winter even in the far North. Since freezing greatly improves their flavor, the best parsnips are harvested in the Spring after they have over-wintered.

The same storage procedures used for other root crops apply to parsnips. They can also be frozen.

One of the best ways to cook parsnips is to French fry them the same way as potatoes. Peel and slice the roots thinly and fry in oil until golden brown. Even people who don't like parsnips enjoy them cooked this way.
Personally, I like parsnips best as wine. Any good wine book will give you the recipe.

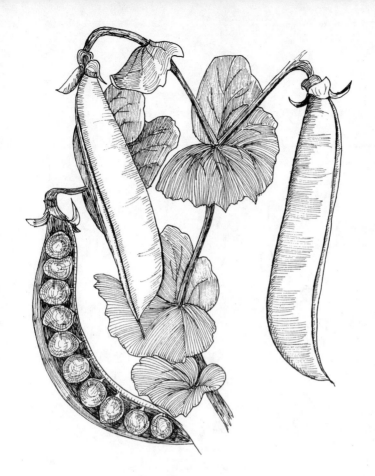

Peas

Peas are one of the all-time garden favorites. Home-grown peas are quite superior to those miserable, store-bought, lifeless things sold as sweet peas. Peas must be eaten quite soon after picking since the sugar rapidly changes to starch. Although they do take a little extra work and are tedious to prepare, they are well worth it.

Besides the sweet pea, another kind which can be grown is the edible podded pea. This one is eaten pod and all much like string beans. They are sometimes called snow peas or sugar peas and are very popular in Chinese cooking. Pick them when young and tender before the peas develop and swell the pod. If they get past this stage they can be shelled out like regular peas.

Peas are natural climbers and all need some kind of support for the vines to climb. Dwarf growing varieties are available and can be grown without a trellis but even with these some sort of support makes picking much easier. A good support can be made by stretching chicken wire between wooden posts. There are also string trellises sold by many seed companies for just this purpose. Another way is to place twiggy brush along the row before the seeds are planted.

The tall-growing varieties (4-5 feet) are heavy yielders compared

to the bush or dwarf
types and can be picked
over a longer period.

peas growing on brush

Peas are very hardy
and should be planted
as soon as the soil can
be prepared. Poor results
are often caused by
planting too late since

they grow best when
the weather is cool. The
best peas we ever grew
were planted during an
early thaw in March
and were snowed on
several times.
   The soil doesn't have
to be heavily fertilized
as with most crops since
peas are quite diligent
at finding their own
food. They also provide
nitrogen for the soil like
other legumes. They won't
grow well in a acid soil
(below pH 5.5) or when
the land is poorly drained.
   Peas are usually
planted in double rows
spaced 8-10 inches apart.
Leave about 2½ feet

between these double rows. First put down the support and plant the seeds 1-2 inches deep on both sides of the trellis. If seeds are planted one inch apart thinning will not be necessary since peas like to be crowded.

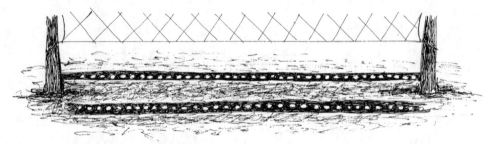

For a continuous harvest plant early, mid-season, and late varieties all at the same time to provide a long picking season. If summers are cool they can be planted again in August to provide a late Fall harvest. Peas should be watered in warm weather. They greatly benefit from a mulch to keep the soil cool and moist.

If peas haven't been grown before in the garden it is a good idea to innoculate the seeds with a nitrogen fixing bacteria the same way as beans. This will help the plants add nitrogen to the soil and also will increase the yield.

Varieties

A great many varieties

have been developed. Some
of the best include:
Sparkle, 60 days, which
grows 15 inches tall and
is ready very early.
Little Marvel, 62 days, grows
18 inches tall and produces
pods near the top where
they are easy to pick.
Lincoln, 67 days, grows 2½
feet tall and is excep-
tionally productive. Wando,
69 days, grows 2½ feet
tall and is the most heat
resistant of all. This
variety will produce good
crops even if planted too
late. Alderman, 74 days,
grows 4-5 feet tall,
producing large 5 inch
pods containing 8-10 peas
of very high quality.

Green Arrow, 68 days, developed in England, is new for 1973. It grows 24-28 inches tall and produces giant-sized pods, containing 9-11 peas. It is highly disease resistant and the pods are produced in pairs near the top for easy picking. It sounds like a winner.

Edible Podded Peas: Dwarf Grey Sugar, 65 days, has attractive red flowers. Mammoth Melting Sugar, 70 days, grows much taller. These are the standard varieties.

Harvesting

Peas are ready to harvest as soon as the pods fill out but before the peas turn tough and the pods start to change color. Several pickings are required since they produce over a long period. Very young peas are extremely sweet and tender and only the home gardener can afford this luxury.

Peas should be eaten or preserved as soon after picking as possible. Edible podded peas are best preserved by freezing.

Peppers

The garden pepper belongs to the Capsicum family which has no relationship at all to the black pepper used at the dinner table. They are closely related to the eggplant and tomato and are grown in much the same way. Basically, there are two types of peppers:

the hot varieties and the
sweet (bell peppers).
 Peppers can be used
in many ways. Red pepper,
or cayenne, is a small
hot variety ground into
a fine powder. Pepper
sauce, or hot sauce, is made
by preserving hot varieties
in a strong brine or in
vinegar. Paprika is made
from ground, dried, sweet
peppers after the seeds
have been removed. All
peppers can be used green
or when they turn red
or yellow at maturity as
with some varieties. A
pepper plant loaded with
red and green fruits
rivals for looks many of
the plants normally grown
as ornamentals.

In the tropics, peppers are true perennials. But in the North, they are grown as tender annuals. The small, fruited kinds are often grown as house plants during the Winter and even these are edible.

A dozen plants of the sweet varieties, and fewer of the hot kinds, should supply the needs of most families. Peppers require a long season to mature and consequently seeds must be started inside 2 months before they are large

Tabasco

enough to set
out. Some
gardeners start
their own
plants, but
pepper plants
can be
purchased
easily at the
greenhouse at

chili

the right time for planting
outside. If you would like
to start your own plants,
grow them at warm
temperatures and don't set
them out until the weather
turns warm and when
danger of frost is past.
    The best soil for
growing peppers in an area
with a short season is
a light, sandy loam. Hot
varieties like a little more

clay in the soil, but both kinds can be grown on a warm, rich loam. The best yields are obtained during seasons of hot, dry weather. Hot varieties sometimes cross-pollinate with sweet peppers which will turn them hot. To prevent this, keep the hot peppers at one end of the garden, away from the sweet peppers.

Space the plants about 18 inches apart with rows spaced 2-3 feet apart. Set the plants a little deeper than they grew

pimento

cayenne

in the pots. The soil level should come to within an inch of the lowest set of leaves. Keep the plants well-watered. One or two feedings with liquid manure when the plants are flowering will help increase productivity.

Varieties

To insure a crop in the North, only the earliest maturing varieties should be grown. Days to maturity are listed from the time plants are set out.

Sweet Varieties: Vinedale, 62 days, developed at the Vineland Experimental Station in Ontario, produces good crops of early peppers on dwarf plants. Canape Hybrid, 62 days, is another good pepper for areas with short seasons. It produces 12-15 peppers on each plant. Staddon's Select, 72 days, produces large, well-shaped peppers early in the season. Other good varieties include Burpee's Early Pimento, 65 days; Sweet Banana, 70 days; and Calwonder, 72 days.

Hot Varieties: Hot Portugal, 64 days, produces hot fruits that are 6 inches long. Hungarian Wax, 65 days. Its 8 inch fruits change from yellow to red at maturity. Not quite as hot as other hot varieties. Long Red Cayenne, 72 days. Its fruits are 5 inches long and easily dried.

Harvesting

Green peppers are ready to pick when they are firm and full-sized. They can also be allowed to ripen and to develop their red color. All peppers are usually picked by snapping off the stems but less injury to the plants will result if the peppers are cut off with a knife. Hot peppers should be allowed to ripen on the plants. They are easily dried by putting the peppers in a warm place until thoroughly dry.

Peppers can be frozen by simply placing them in plastic bags or containers in the freezer. Blanching is not necessary. Frozen peppers will not have the crispness needed for salads but are ideal for flavoring many dishes.

Potatoes

The potato is the world's leading vegetable crop. Annual world production has passed 12 billion bushels and comes close to wheat in total value. The original potato is native to South America, and is related to the tomato, also eggplant, and tobacco. It differs mainly from these others

due to its habit of
producing tubers on
underground stems. Potatoes
need a long, cool, growing
season as witnessed by the
fact that most potatoes
are grown here commercially
in only the northern
states and in Canada.
   Any good soil will
produce potatoes. An ideal
soil is well-drained and
deeply worked, with a
pH between 5 and 6. An
acid soil is best because
it discourages the
formation of potato scab,
a fungus disease. For this
reason the soil should
not be limed. Scab produces
unsightly marks on the
potatoes but it doesn't
affect their eating quality.

potato scab

Potatoes are not grown from seed but from pieces of potato. Try to purchase certified seed potatoes as these are free from disease. Potatoes bought at the store have often been treated with chemicals to prevent them from sprouting in storage. They are totally unfit for seed purposes. Seed potatoes can be purchased at many farm and garden supply stores, or potato sets can be ordered from many mail order seed companies.

Eight to ten pounds of seed potatoes will plant 100 feet of row and should yield 3-4 bushels. Small seed potatoes can be planted whole or larger ones cut into 3-4 pieces, each one with at least one "eye" or sprout. If the potatoes are going to be cut, it is best done about one week before planting to give the cut surfaces a chance to form callouses. Seed potatoes can also be left

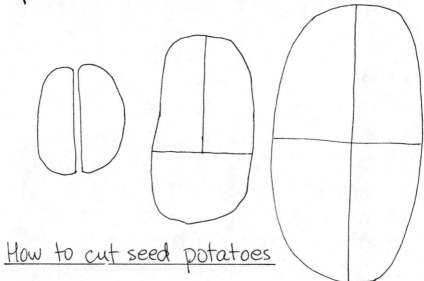

How to cut seed potatoes

in the sun to "green" for a few weeks prior to planting. This develops short, green sprouts and causes more rapid growth and earlier yield.

Large potatoes can also be planted whole but if only a limited amount of seed is available or when seed is very expensive it is probably more advantageous to cut them up.

Planting can be done as early as the soil can be prepared. The length of time needed to form tubers varies from season to season as well as from place to place. Seed potatoes are planted 1-2 inches deep in heavy, clay soils and up to 4 inches deep on lighter, sandier soils. The seed potatoes are placed 12 inches apart in rows spaced 24-30 inches apart. Many organic gardeners have had excellent results by planting potatoes under a mulch of 10-12 inches of loose hay. The potato plants are able to grow through this mulch but the weeds can't penetrate and are killed. We have been using this system and it really works. After the potatoes are planted and covered with a mulch, nothing has to be done until harvest time.

The Colorado Potato Beetle can be troublesome at times, eating the foliage and indirectly reducing yield. The adult beetle is about ½ inch long and has 10 black, longitudinal stripes over a yellow body. It deposits orange eggs on the underside of the leaves and these hatch into orange caterpillar-like insects. The best way to prevent damage is to look over the plants once a week and knock the insects into a small can of kerosene.

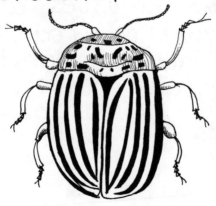

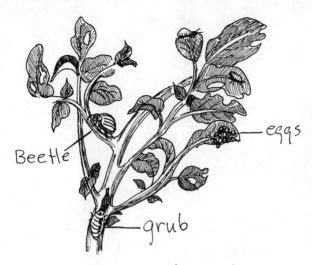

Beetle

eggs

grub

<u>Varieties</u>

Early varieties mature in about 2½-3 months. Late varieties take up to 4 months. Irish Cobbler, early, is an old, popular, standard variety. Kennebec, midseason, is blight resistant. Norgold Russet, early, is a good baking type, cooking up dry and mealy. Red Pontiac, mid-season, is a red-skinned potato and a heavy producer. Russet Burbank, midseason, is a variety often sold as the "Idaho" potato, not a heavy yielder. Katahdin, late, is fairly disease resistant.

Some novelty potatoes you might want to try are Yellow Fingerlings and German Purple! These grow to about the size and shape of a finger. German Purple is blue-skinned but yellow-fleshed.

Harvesting

Early "new" potatoes can be due after the plant blossoms. These can be harvested by gently searching under the plant and carefully removing as many potatoes as needed,

leaving the plants to grow.
    The main crop should
be left to mature until
the vines wither and can
be left in the ground
for several weeks more,
if desired. Most of the
tubers develop about 3-4
inches below the soil.
They should be dug when
the soil is dry and placed
in containers. They must
be stored in darkness to
            prevent them
            from turning
            green, when they
            develop a poison-
            ous substance
            called
                solanine.

Green potatoes are not fit to eat. The storage place should be humid with a temperature below 40° F. but should not be below freezing.

<u>Radish</u>

The radish is a
favorite with home
gardeners since it is so
easily grown and is ready
to eat in only 3-4 weeks.
They are a wonderful item
to include in a child's
garden to teach them the
joys of gardening,
possibly initiating a

lifelong hobby. This was the first vegetable I ever planted, way back in grade school, in cheese boxes on a sunny windowsill.

Radishes can be grown anywhere in the country and on all types of soils, but a light, rich loam is considered best. They are usually planted in the same row and at the same time with other slow-growing vegetables to mark the area and to help break any crust which might form over the row. They are ready to eat at about the same time the slower-growing vegetables are just coming up and do not hinder them in the least.

Radishes are planted very early in the Spring to avoid growing in hot weather. A quickly available plant food such as compost or well-rotted manure (never fresh manure) and rock phosphate should be lightly dug into the area where the plants will be grown.

Two types of radishes are planted. The Spring radishes and the very large Winter radishes. The early, round, red radishes mature in 20-30 days. The large Winter radishes, planted in late Summer, should mature in 60 days, around the time of the first frost.

Spring radish seeds should be planted ½ inch deep in rows spaced only 10 inches apart and thinned to an inch apart within the row. Successive plantings can be made 10 days to two weeks apart but should be discontinued when the weather turns hot. All radishes must be grown quickly which calls for an abundant supply of water. Slow growing radishes will be hot and pithy.

Varieties

<u>Spring radishes</u>: Cherry Belle, 22 days; French Breakfast, 23 days, an olive

shaped, red radish with a white tip; Champion, 26 days, grows very large without becoming pithy, our favorite; White Icicle, 27 days, a fine, white radish which grows about 5 inches long.

Winter radishes: Long Black Spanish, Round Black Spanish, China Rose Winter, New Celestial, and Sakurajima which grows to enormous size and has a fine flavor. All mature in about 60 days.

Harvesting

Radishes are harvested as soon as the roots reach edible size. The Spring varieties become hot if left too long after they mature. The Winter varieties can be stored for several months in a cool place packed in earth or sand.

Winter radishes are very popular in Japan and are served in many ways. They can also be dried by shredding them thinly and putting them in a warm place. They are also eaten raw or cooked much the same as turnips. They are especially nice lightly breaded and fried in oil.

Rhubarb

Rhubarb, or pie plant
as it is sometimes called,
is a hardy perennial.
Although a vegetable, the
thick leaf stalks are used
as fruit. Since the plants
are so long-lived, they
should be planted at one
side of the garden where

they can remain undisturbed.
The delicious, tart, red stalks are made into sauces, jams, stewed with other fruits (especially strawberries). And who can resist a good rhubarb pie?

Rhubarb is one of the first plants to come up in the Spring, even when the ground is still icy-cold. The plants are very cold resistant, in fact, they grow best where the ground freezes solid each Winter. Rhubarb is an amiable plant, seldom bothered by insects or disease, doing well on all types of soils.

Plants are usually not grown from seed, but

from root divisions which
can be obtained from
any seed company or
from an established patch.
Each division should have
at least one eye or bud,
preferably two. In the
North, planting is done
only in the Spring, but in
milder regions Fall planting
is sometimes practiced.
Roots are planted
3-4 inches deep with plants
spaced 4 feet apart in
all directions. Unless the
soil is very rich, work in
generous amounts of
manure. In addition, plants
will benefit from a mulch
of manure applied in the
Spring and again at the
end of the harvest period.

It is hardly possible to over-fertilize them, the richer the soil the more tender the stalks, and the longer the harvest will last.

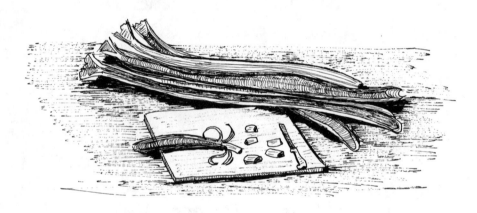

Varieties

The common, green-stalked rhubarb grown in grandma's day has been greatly improved. Newer, deep red varieties are available and these should be the first choice of discriminating gardeners. The best of the newer varieties include: MacDonald, Valentine, and Canada Red.

Harvesting

Stalks should not be harvested the year they are planted. Only moderate cutting should be done the second year to build up strong plants. The stalks should be pulled — not cut, by pulling down and away from the plants. Always leave a few stalks on the plants. A harvest period of 8-10 weeks can be expected

after the plants are well
established. Only the leaf
stalks should be eaten,
never the leaves, as
these contain oxalic acid
which is toxic. Seed stalks
should not be allowed
to grow since they will
sap too much energy
from the plants. These are
easily identifiable since
they are hollow.

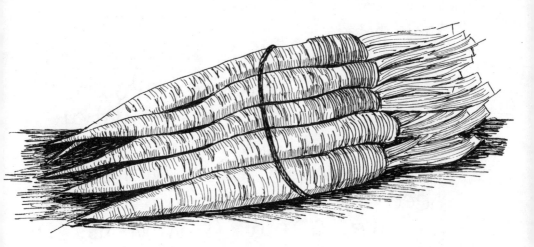

<u>Salsify</u>

Salsify is also called "the vegetable oyster" because of its flavor. Perhaps this is a slight exaggeration. Nevertheless, it does have an agreeable taste. The roots may be boiled, sautéed, or made into mock oyster stew. They can also be cooked by substituting them in any parsnip or carrot

recipe.
Salsify is very hardy. It can be grown anywhere in the country. The roots, which grow to a length of 8 inches, need a long season to mature, about 4 months. They are grown and cared for practically the same way as parsnips. Seeds are planted in rows spaced 14 inches apart and the plants are then thinned to 3-4 inches apart in the row.

Varieties

Mammoth Sandwich Island, 120 days, is the most popular variety,

in fact, it's the only
one I've seen.

Harvesting

The hardy roots
may be left in the ground
all winter and used in
the Spring. Or part of the
crop may be stored like
any other root crop.
Personally, I prefer
dandelion roots!

<u>Spinach</u>

Spinach grows best during the cool days of early Spring and Fall, quickly going to seed when the weather turns hot. Experiments indicate that the day length also has an effect on seed stalk formation. This explains why some varieties go to seed when planted in the Spring but not when planted in the Fall. The "long standing" varieties usually extend the harvest period by 2-3 weeks.

The soil should be rich and moist yet well drained. The best pH is between 6 and 7. When lower, plants will grow poorly, if at all.

Seeds are planted ½ inch deep in rows spaced 12-15 inches apart. Plants should be thinned when they are starting to crowd, by removing and eating the largest ones each time. Continue thinning until the plants are 4-5 inches apart, which will allow them to grow to full size. When they are about half grown, or about 3 weeks old, we mulch them and also apply a high nitrogen fertilizer such as blood meal or soya meal. This helps to produce large, tender leaves.

New Zealand Spinach is not a true spinach but it is useful for summer greens, since the plants are very heat resistant. This variety grows very large, often 3-4 feet across and 1 or 2 feet high. Its seeds are very hard and should be soaked for several hours or overnight before planting. Only the tips of the branches are harvested when 4-5 inches long. Plants are spaced 1½ - 2 feet apart in rows spaced 2½ feet apart. The taste resembles spinach to some extent and can be used the same way.

Varieties

Winter Bloomsdale, 45 days, is a good blight resistant type. Viking, 46 days, has smooth easy-to-wash leaves. America, 50 days, is another good long standing variety. Hybrid No. 7, 42 days, grows quickly but goes to seed as soon as the weather turns warm. New Zealand

Spinach, 70 days, may be harvested all season.

Harvesting

The plants can be used from the time they are half grown until just before the seed stalks develop. Cut the plants just below the bottom set of leaves. Remove all the dead and discolored leaves and wash the plants thoroughly to remove any dirt and sand.

Squashes & Pumpkins

Squashes and pumpkins are closely related botanically and are grouped together because their cultural requirements are identical. They are one of the few American vegetables and were said to be served at the first Thanksgiving dinner in Plymouth. They are a typical New England

favorite.
   Their cultural
requirements are similar
to melons, but they mature
quicker and are grown
in all parts of the
country and in many parts
of Canada. They take up
a lot of room in the
small garden but can be
grown as a companion
to corn if space is
limited. (See corn.)
   Any good well-drained
soil will produce good
crops if weather conditions
are favorable. They are
easily injured by early
frosts and planting should
be delayed until the
weather is warm and
settled. Although not

commonly practiced, they may be started early inside about a month before outside planting time.

Squashes are divided into two types: the Summer squash and the Winter squash. The Summer varieties mature quickly in about 50-60 days. They have soft skin and are not stored like Winter squash and pumpkins. Winter squash have a hard rind and are allowed to fully mature on the vine.

Winter squash and pumpkins are planted in hills spaced 5x5 feet apart. There are, however, new, smaller-growing, bush varieties of Winter squash and pumpkins and these may be planted somewhat closer.

Summer squash grows on a bush and needs much less space. They are usually planted in rows spaced 3 feet apart with the plants thinned to 1½-2 feet apart within the row. If planted in hills, allow 3 feet in all directions and thin to the two best plants in each hill. Only 2-3 plants of the Summer varieties are needed since they are such abundant yielders and especially since the fruits can not be stored.

Varieties

Summer Squash:
Zucchini Elite, Aristocrat Hybrid (new for 1973, Zucchini type), Early Prolific Straightneck (yellow fruits), Seneca Butterbar (hybrid yellow), Cocozelle (Italian Marrow), St. Pat Scallop (patty pan type). All mature in approximately 50-60 days.

Winter Squash:
Buttercup, 105 days, whose fruits weigh about 4-5 lbs. This is our favorite variety. Another favorite is Gold Nugget, 85 days, which grows on a bush, taking up very little

garden space.
Each plant of this variety produces about one half dozen squashes, weighing 1½ - 2 lbs. each. Blue Hubbard, 120 days, grows very large, 15 lbs. or more, and is a good keeper. Waltham Butternut, 85 days, is an improved butternut type. Acorn and Bush Table Queen, 80 days.

Pumpkins: Small Sugar, 100 days, is the famous New England Pie Pumpkin. Cinderella, 102 days, produces full-sized pumpkins on small, bush type vines. Spookie, 110 days, is good for an all-purpose pumpkin for jack-o-lanterns and pies. Connecticut Field, 115 days, grows to 20 lbs. and

larger but is not as good
for eating as the other
varieties.

Harvesting

Summer squash are
harvested when very
young and tender. If
the fruits are not easily
punctured with the thumb-
nail, they are too old to
eat. Try to harvest them
when small, just after the
blossom falls off for the
best quality.

Winter squash and
pumpkins are allowed to
ripen thoroughly on the
vines. They should be
harvested when fully ripe
but before they have been
frosted. They should be
cut from the vines with

a portion of the stem attached. Handle them carefully to prevent bruising since injured fruits decay rapidly and are useless for storage.

Storage

Summer squash are not stored. However, they may be frozen or canned. Winter squash and pumpkins will keep for many months if they are in good condition and fully mature. Their storage requirements are completely different from other crops. After the fruits are harvested they are cured at a temperature of 70-85 degrees, which hardens

the shells. After 2 weeks
of curing, the fruits
should be moved to a
dry place with a temp-
erature between 50-65
degrees, where they will
keep in fine condition
for many months.

Look over the squashes
and pumpkins and quickly
use any fruits that
show signs of mold or
decay. Incidentally, some
of the best "pumpkin" pies
are made with squash
instead of with pumpkins.

Strawberries

Of all the fruits, strawberries are the quickest to yield a crop and the easiest to grow. Even the smallest garden can accomodate 50-75 plants, which should supply the needs of a family of 3 or 4. Under average conditions each plant can be expected to produce

about a quart of berries.
Strawberries will do well on a wide range of soil types, even an acid soil will produce good crops. Always start out with strong, healthy plants from a reliable nursery or, preferably, from a nursery which specializes in strawberries. Try to plant them on land that has been under cultivation for at least one year, which helps to destroy deep-rooted, perennial weeds and white grubs usually found in sods.

Prepare the soil well by spading or rototilling and incorporate large amounts of organic matter.

Manure is undoubtedly the best fertilizer and soil conditioner, but compost, lawn clippings, leaf mold, or peat moss will also bring fine results.

I can hardly over-emphasize the importance of starting out with good plants. Even if a well-meaning neighbor offers some plants from his patch I would politely thank him but refuse to plant them. Most states have a program that rigorously inspects and certifies that the plants you receive are free from viruses, root diseases, and all insect pests. Good strawberry plants are cheap, costing about $6.-$7.

per hundred. Usually 25 plants of one variety is the smallest quantity sold.

Early Spring is the best time to plant here in the North. They may also be planted later, but the results are never as certain. If the plants arrive before the land is ready, open the package and, if the roots seem dry, soak them in water for an hour. Then return them to the original package and place them in the refrigerator, not the freezer.

There are several planting systems used by commercial growers and home gardeners. The easiest for the home gardener is the matted row. Plants are set 2 feet apart in rows 3-4 feet apart. Runner plants are allowed to grow in all directions and to fill in the rows. This system produces the highest yields.

Another method we have tried is the hill system. This produces the largest-sized berries but involves a little more work. Plants are set 18 inches apart in all directions in beds which contain 3 or 4 rows. All the runners are removed as soon as they appear and only the original plants are allowed to produce.

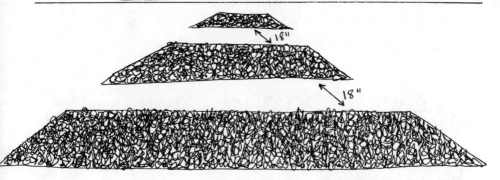

<u>matted row system</u>

The plants are set
in holes large enough to
allow the roots to be
spread out without crowding.
Set them deep enough
so that the roots are not
exposed, but make sure the
crown is not buried.

With all systems,
remove all the flowers the
same season they are
planted, and do not allow

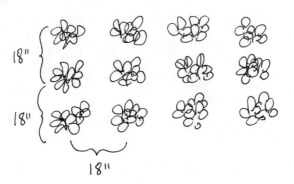

<u>hill system</u>

them to produce any fruit. Weeding and cultivating should be done regularly, since deep-rooted weeds will be hard to remove once the plants are established. If the land has been well prepared and fertilized, no other feeding should be necessary. But if plants are making a poor growth, an extra feeding of soya meal, fish fertilizer, or compost, should be done

correct planting depth

only in August since this is the time that the fruit buds form for the next season. Watering may be necessary if a long, dry period follows planting.

Most strawberry growers protect the plants with a mulch of 3-4 inches of hay, sawdust, or pine needles. This is applied when the weather turns cold, but before the ground freezes. We have never found it necessary here since snow comes early, which is the best protection of all.

Remove the mulch from on top of the plants in the Spring before new leaves start to turn yellow.

Work the mulch between the rows and plants to keep the berries clean and to prevent them from rotting, which might occur if the berries come in contact with bare soil.

Varieties

Different varieties are adapted to various climates, and soils, some are good for eating fresh, others are good for shipping, freezing, and some are especially disease resistant. There is no one perfect variety. Try several and see which you like the most and which grows best in your area.

Some good varieties
for cold climates include:
Catskill, Redcoat (especially
good for very cold regions),
Sparkle, Fairfax, Premier,
and Midway. Other fine
varieties to try are:
Redglow, Sunrise, Surecrop,
and Guardian.

Harvesting

Wait until the berries
are bright red all over
before picking them. If
they show any signs of
green or white, leave them
for another day or two.
After picking don't let
them sit in the sun too
long.
Strawberries may be
fruited one, two, three, or

sometimes four years if the plants are unusually healthy. At the end of the harvest, thoroughly weed the bed, cut off all the tops of the strawberry plants (if they show any signs of disease) by using a lawn mower set high, and remove all the excess plants in the matted row system. Leave only 2 or 3 plants per square foot. It is usually better, however, to fruit them only 1 or 2 years and to start another bed in a new location using fresh plants.

<u>Everbearing Strawberries:</u>
These are not as satisfactory as the June bearers. They require a

very fertile soil, more water, constant attention, and they almost never equal the yield of the June bearing types. They do have the advantage of producing a few berries every day if conditions are right, but since we freeze our surplus it hardly seems worthwhile to fool with them. They produce few runners and are best grown using the hill system. Everbearers are usually fruited only one season before the planting is dug up.

But if weeds are kept under control and the plants are healthy, they may be kept for another year. Try Ozark Beauty, Ogallala, and Geneva.

<u>Tomatoes</u>

The tomato, or "love apple", is one of the most popular vegetables and is grown in nearly all home gardens. Although tomatoes have been grown for centuries as an ornamental, they were considered poisonous until the middle

of the 19th century.
The tomato is a warm season plant and will not withstand frost. Do not plant out too early unless you plan to protect them with hot-caps (small plastic tents) or portable coldframes.

They require a long season to mature, so plants should be started early inside or purchased at the greenhouse. Start the seeds during the first week in April and give them the same care as eggplants.

The tomato is one of the heaviest yielders for the space it occupies. Ten to 15 plants produce all the tomatoes we can possibly use, including

enough for canning a
winter's supply of sauce,
paste, and stewed tomatoes.
The plants are set
deep, up to the first set
of leaves, since roots will
form all along the buried
part of the stem. Plants
are spaced 4-5 feet apart
if you let them sprawl,
as we do. Or they may be
set 2-3 feet apart if
they are staked and
pruned to a single stem.
Although staking requires
more work, it does save
garden space and often
results in an earlier yield
and larger fruit. Plants
allowed to grow naturally
will usually yield more
per plant but staking allows
more plants to be grown

in the same area.

Gardeners have invented all sorts of methods of staking plants. Some use wire cylinders, racks, trellises, and fences, but the most common practice is to use stakes measuring 1x2's or 2x2's about 6-8 feet long. We usually go into the woods and cut a few sapplings in the early Spring. They do just as well. These are driven into the ground, 18-24 inches, a few inches away from the plants. Some gardeners pinch off the top of the plant when it reaches the top of the stake.

Staked plants are usually pruned to only one

stem, sometimes two. All
of the shoots which grow
in the axils of the leaves
(called suckers) are
removed when small, less
than 2-3 inches.
The plants are tied
to the stakes
when they are
one foot
high with
soft
twine or
strips of
cloth. This
should be
done carefully
so that the
stems are not cut by the
twine.
 Tomatoes are not
too fussy about the soil,
but for added insurance

suckers

stake

we usually place a good-sized shovelful of manure under each plant. They do require a sunny location and must be protected against those early June frosts so common here in northern Vermont. Keep a close watch on the thermometer if the temperature at sunset is near 45° or below, since frost is likely where we are, especially if the skies are clear and the wind still.

Varieties

If you grow your own plants from seed, you have a wide choice of over 50

varieties offered by seeds-
men. Most greenhouses
usually grow only a half
dozen kinds of the most
popular varieties. Some
varieties produce fruit
weighing 2-3 lbs. each and
others produce fruit no
larger than a marble.
Kids especially love these
bite-sized treats.

Some of the better
new varieties combine
high yield, extra fine
quality, and disease
resistance: Burpee's Big
Early Hybrid, 62 days,
Springset, 67 days; Moreton
Hybrid, 70 days; Jet Star,
72 days; Burpee's Delicious,
77 days; Burpee's Big Boy
Hybrid, 78 days. The best

small fruited tomato we've grown is Small Fry Hybrid, 68 days.

For a yellow tomato, try Sunray, 72 days, and Jubilee, also 72 days.

Roma VF, 76 days, and San Marzano, 80 days, are grown especially for paste and canning whole.

All days to maturity are calculated from the time plants are set out.

Harvesting

Everyone knows the best tomatoes have been allowed to ripen on the vine. In late fall, all full-sized tomatoes should be brought in before they become frosted. If they are stored at a cool temperature, around 45°, and each fruit wrapped individually in newspaper, fresh tomatoes may be enjoyed until early Winter. At higher temperatures the fruits will ripen much quicker.

A good way to use up an extra large surplus is to make tomato paste. Just place as many tomatoes as you have in a large pot, turn the heat real low, and let simmer for about one hour. It helps to crush a few tomatoes to get the juices running. Then put everything through a large strainer or food mill and return the liquid portion to the pot. Discard the

seeds and skin to the
compost pile as these
are of no further use.
Continue simmering until
the right consistency is
reached. You may freeze
the paste or can it in
a boiling water bath
for 45 minutes.

Turnips and Rutabagas

These two vegetables
are closely related and
require the same general
care. Turnips are quick
growing and mature in 40-
60 days. Rutabagas, also
called Swedish Turnips or
Swedes, grow much larger
and take a month longer
to mature. Both are hardy,

cool season crops and may be planted in the early Spring or, more commonly, in mid to late Summer to mature in the Fall.

Some varieties of turnips are grown especially for their tops. These are the famous turnip greens. But any variety can be used for this purpose.

Rutabagas are grown commercially in the northern states and, to a much greater extent, in Canada. While they are similar in appearance to the turnip, rutabagas have a larger, denser root and the leaves are not hairy (and are usually not eaten). The flavor of the rutabaga is superior to the turnip, being sweeter and not as coarsely textured. They are excellent keepers, much better than turnips, and often last us well into the Spring.

One packet of seed each of turnips and rutabagas will supply the needs of most families. Seeds germinate quickly and the plants grow rapidly. Seeds are planted where the crop is to mature, almost never transplanted. Prepare the soil deeply as for other root crops and fertilize in the same way. Wood ashes are helpful. Place a sprinkling along the row to supply some extra potash and to discourage the root maggot which sometimes tunnels into the roots. Turnip seeds are planted ½ inch deep in rows 12-15 inches apart. Thin the plants to stand 3-4 inches apart. Rutabagas need at least 16 inches between rows and the plants thinned to 6 inches apart. Both are hardy and are not injured by Fall frost.

Varieties

<u>Turnips</u>: Purple Top White Globe, 55 days, has been the standard, all-purpose turnip for many years. Early Purple Top

Milan, 45 days, is another popular early turnip which produces flattened roots growing 3-4 inches across. Foliage or Shogoin produces a dense growth of leaves in 30 days and roots in 2 months. Tokyo Cross Hybrid will produce roots in only 35 days and is resistant to disease.

Rutabagas: Purple Top Yellow, 90 days, is purple at the top and yellow at the bottom and has yellow flesh. Long Island, 90 days, is quite similar. Macomber, 90 days, is an old popular variety which has white flesh instead of yellow like other varieties.

Harvesting

Turnips and rutabagas are best harvested before they grow to full size. They are much sweeter then, since older roots get tough and stringy. Rutabagas, though they grow much larger, should still be harvested when young to provide the best eating quality. Both of them are stored like any other root crop.

Planting Chart

Cool Season Crops: can be planted early, as soon as soil is workable.

Artichoke, Jerusalem
Asparagus
Broccoli
Brussel Sprouts
Cabbage
Carrots
Cauliflower
Celeriac
Celery
Celtuce
Corn Salad
Endive
Kale

Kohlrabi
Lettuce
Leek
Mustard
Onions
Parsley
Parsnips
Peas
Radish
Rutabagas
Salsify
Spinach
Turnips

Warm Season Crops: plant when weather is warm + settled.

Beans (all Kinds)   Peppers
Cantaloupes   Pumpkins
Corn   Squash
Cucumber   Tomatoes
Eggplant   Watermelon
New Zealand
        Spinach

Late Crops: can be planted in Midsummer for Fall harvests.

Beets   Lettuce
Chinese Cabbage   Mustard
Carrots   Radish (all Kinds)
Endive   Rutataga
Kale   Spinach
Kohlrabi   Turnips

Sources of Supply

<u>Seedsmen</u>:

Breck's of Boston, 200 Breck Bldg.
  Boston, Mass. 02210.

Burgess Seed and Plant Co.,
  Galesburg, Michigan 49053.

W.A. Burpee Co., 370 Burpee Bldg.,
  Philadelphia, Pa. 19132.

Farmer Seed & Nursery Co.,
  Faribault, Minnesota, 55021.

Henry Field Seed & Nursery Co.,
  Shenandoah, Iowa, 51601.

Gurney Seed & Nursery Co.,
  Yankton, S. Dakota, 57078.

Joseph Harris Co., Inc., Moreton
  Farm, Rochester, N.Y., 14624.

J.W. Jung Seed Co., Randolph,
  Wiconsin, 53956.

Earl May Seed & Nursery Co.,
  6032 Elm Street, Shenandoah,
  Iowa, 51601.

Nichols Garden Nursery, 1190
  N. Pacific Highway, Albany,
  Oregon, 97321.

Kitazawa Seed Co., 356 West Taylor St.,
    San Jose, Calif. 95110.
L.L. Olds Seed Co., Box 1069,
    Madison, Wisconsin, 53701.
George W. Park Seed Co., Inc.,
    Greenwood, South Carolina
    29547.
R.H. Shumway, Rockford, Illinois
    61101.
Stokes Seeds Inc., 86 Exchange St.
    Buffalo, N.Y., 14205.
Vesey's Seeds Ltd., York,
    Prince Edward Island,
    Canada.

Herbs

Hemlock Hills Herb Farm, Litchfield,
    Connecticut, 06759.
Merry Gardens, Camden, Maine,
    04843.
Nichols Garden Nursery 1190
        North Pacific Highway,
        Albany, Oregon, 97321.
Sunnybrook Farms Nusery, 9448
        Mayfield Road, Chestertown,
        Ohio, 44026.

Meadowbrook Herb Garden, Rt. 138,
   Wyoming, R.I., 02898
Green Herb Gardens, Green, R.I.
   02927.

Soil Test Kits

La Motte Chemical Products Co.,
   Chestertown, Maryland.
Sudbury Laboratory Inc.,
   Box 1076, Sudbury, Mass.
   01776.

Plant Growing Lights

Gro-Lux bulbs, manufactured by
   Sylvania Lighting Products,
   60 Boston Street, Salem,
   Mass.
Plant-Gro lights, made by Westing-
   house Electric Corporation,
   Bloomfield, New Jersey.
These lamps are usually available
through large mail order firms,

such as Sears Roebuck and
Montgomery Ward.

Beneficial Insects

Lakeland Nurseries, Hanover, Pa.
    17331.
Bio-Control Co., Rt.2, Box 2397,
    Auburn, California, 95603.
The Vitova Co., Inc., Biological
    Control Division, P.O. Box 745,
    Rialto, California, 92376.
Mincemoyer's Nursery, R.D. 5,
    Box 379, New Prospect Road,
    Jackson, New Jersey, 08527.
Schnoor's Sierra Bug Co.,
    P.O. Box 114, Rough and
    Ready, California, 95975.

Selected Bibliography

Companion Plants, Helen Philbrick &
    Richard Gregg, The Devin-
    Adair Co., New York, 1966.
Complete Book of Composting,
    J.I. Rodale & Staff. Rodale
    Books Inc., Emmaus, Pa., 1971.
Encyclopedia of Organic Gardening,
    J.I. Rodale & Staff. Rodale
    Books Inc., Emmaus, Pa., 1959.
Fluorescent Light Gardening,
    Elaine C. Cherry. D. Van
    Nostrand Co., Inc., New York, 1965.
Gardening Without Poisons, Beatrice
    Trum Hunter, Houghton
    Mifflin Co., Boston, 1964.
Gardening Without Work, Ruth
    Stout, The Devin-Adair Co.,
    New York, 1969.
Herb Gardening In Five Seasons,
    Adelma G. Simmons, D. Van
    Nostrand Co. Inc., New York, 1964.

Herbs: Their Culture and Uses,
    Rosetta E. Clarkson, The
    Macmillan Co., New York, 1942.
How to Grow Vegetables and Fruits
    By the Organic Method,
    J.I. Rodale + Staff, Rodale
    Books Inc., Emmaus, Pa., 1961.
Manual of Cultivated Plants, L.H.
    Bailey, The Macmillan Co.,
    New York, 1924.
Pfeiffer Garden Book, Bio-Dynamics
    In the Home Garden, Bio-
    Dynamic Farming + Gardening
    Association, Inc., Stroudsburg,
    Pa., 1967.
Ruth Stout No Work Garden Book,
    Ruth Stout + Richard Clemence,
    Rodale Press, Inc., Emmaus, Pa.
Silent Spring, Rachel Carson,
    Houghton Mifflin Co., Boston,
    Mass., 1962.
The Soil and Health, Sir Albert
    Howard, The Devin-Adair Co.,
    New York.
Step-By-Step To Organic Vegetable
    Growing, Samuel R. Ogden,
    Rodale Press, Inc., Emmaus, Pa.